the Magnificent

—— The Christ of heaven revealed ——

Jesus

Walking in intimacy

JOHAN DEN HARTOGH & KEN GOTT

The Magnificent Jesus
By Johan den Hartogh & Ken Gott

Published by Public Transformation
Rijswijk, The Netherlands

Graphic design
Sander Suk

ISBN 9789493274136
NUR 707

(Also available as e-book: ISBN 9789493274181)

First published, november 2024

Public Transformation – Tell your Story!

Photo credits
Chapter 1 www.freepik.com image 18270252 | Chapter 2 www.dreamstime.com image 200022859
Chapter 3 www..shutterstock.com image 2130665909 | Chapter 4 www.unsplash.com image F55HaVWQ
Chapter 5 www.photodune.net image 27143749 | Chapter 6 www.pelago.com image pelprlzoq-private-romantic-sunset-cruise-in-sittee-river-village-hopkins/ | Chapter 7 iStock image 145163012-5305167
Chapter 8 www.unsplash.com image 4I6VIZI79HE | Chapter 9 www.unsplash.com image 4EeVLcCJfiM
Chapter 10 www.iStoc.com image 167532012-253214

Table of Contents

Foreword

Hewn from ancient lands where the lingering scents of past revivals still pervade the rocky landscapes, prayer patriarch Ken Gott and his spiritual son Johan den Hartogh, rooted in that history, present a new manuscript: *The Magnificent Jesus - The Christ of Heaven Revealed*. A new generation of readers will catch that scent, behold the beauty of Christ, hunger for God, and return to the Rock from which they were hewn. There is hope for a tree, even when it has been cut down, for at the scent of water, new shoots will spring forth.

My life has been wonderfully knit to the soul of Ken Gott over the years. I first heard of him in the revivals of the 90's where the news spread of the awesome outbreak of the Spirit in Sunderland, North England, the very town of Smith Wigglesworth's revivals decades before. Ken was the father in that furnace of the Spirits fire.

Then we sovereignly connected in a small 24/7 house of prayer in Pasadena, California, where our hearts united with the vision of establishing day-and-night prayer across the nations. From the house of prayer he later founded in Sunderland, the fire on the altar of his heart has never gone out. Years ago, during my time in the Netherlands, I met Johan. We soon realised that we had both established a Justice House of Prayer and shared the same calling: to pray for the abolition of abortion in our respective countries.

Now, from the deep and rich heart history of Ken and his spiritual son Johan, who have both lived in the Presence of God, comes a book unveiling and magnifying the glorious names of Christ as revealed in the book of Revelation. This unveiling will fuel the fires of the church's prayer life, kindle the Bride's longing for the Bridegroom, equip God's people to stand firm in these evil days, and extend the dominion of the King.

Jesus' great apostolic manifesto, "Upon this rock (the revelation of Christ) I will build My church, and the gates of hell will not prevail against it," was set into motion by Peter's explosive revelation: "You are the Christ, the Son of the Living God!" From this one powerful revelation of the name *Christos*, Jesus began to build His Ecclesia. Through the dynamic revelations of the names of Christ in this book, may Jesus rename and reframe you, and use you to further build His end-time Ecclesia, His Ruling Body of Prayer in the nations. As you read, there will be awe-inspiring moments, and Heaven will declare over you, just as Jesus declared over Peter, "Flesh and blood has not revealed this to you, but My Father who is in heaven!"

> *There is a river flowing from the throne,*
> *Crystal clear and beautiful, with power all its own,*
> *Proceeding from the Father, mediated through the Son,*
> *God the Holy Spirit has now come upon us.*

Come, read *The Magnificent Jesus*, and immerse yourself in the ancient underground rivers of Christological revelation that flow from the Throne. May this book ignite the glorious river of the Holy Spirit to erupt and flow out to all who are thirsty, and to the thirsty lands of the earth.

I am so grateful to the Father in Heaven, who has given us a father and a spiritual son on earth to bring us this book of revelations of Christ. The same revelations of Christ that were so vital to the early church are even more desperately needed today by us, those upon whom the end of the ages has come. Indeed, they are essential for the fulfilment of that glorious final book of *Revelation*!

Lou Engle

Preface

At the beginning of this book, we invite you to pray with us, which Paul writes about in the letter to the Ephesians (Eph. 1:17).

> *Father God,*
> *As I read this book, will you give me the spirit of wisdom and wisdom and revelation.*
> *So that I, together with many others, will get to know Jesus better! In Jesus' name, Amen*

This book is all about our union with Christ! The most important thing is that we begin to look upon Him and start the practice of gazing upon Him. Together, we can explore the depth, height, length, and breadth of the knowledge of Him. His love and power are endless.

It is all about Jesus. Everything will be brought under Him as the head. World history culminates in Him. He is the ultimate fulfillment. Now it is time to discover all the treasures the Father has placed in Him, so that we might discover and even tremble at this unique, powerful, loving, and awe-inspiring personality. Eternal life is to know Him, and there is a world-wide longing to know and love Him.

The Bridegroom is coming back very soon, and the wedding day is approaching when we will sit with Him at the marriage feast of the Lamb, for His bride has made herself ready. In preparation for that day, we need to make ourselves ready and spend time together, knowing everything about each other.

Let us link arms, minds, and hearts in unity to say, "Jesus, we want to know everything about You." This is our preparation for the wedding day, but before that day, we want to see Your church restored. We desire that the

Ekklesia – His Body – be fully active, which begins by focusing on the Head, the Christ of Heaven – **The Magnificent Jesus**.

In order to reflect His glory, we need to spend quality time with Jesus. The greatest pursuit of the human heart is to know the One who made me and to be fascinated by Him. Look at Jesus and be forever changed!
Are you prepared today to go on this journey?

> *Blessed is the man whose strength is in You,*
> *Whose heart is set on pilgrimage.*
> *(Psalm 84:5)*

Johan den Hartogh & Ken Gott

Introduction

Our desire for the church is a deep relationship with Jesus through the Holy Spirit. We can no longer live on wonderful projects, grand festivals, or bookshelves full of theology. We no longer desire mere religious practice, but we want to truly know Him. It is precisely during this time that the deepest question of the heart arises: "How strong is my connection with Him? How well do we know each other?"

This book, the first of three, is about various characteristics of Jesus in the book of Revelation aimed at helping us get to know Jesus better and to prepare us for the return of the Son. In the first chapters of the Bible book of Revelation, Jesus walks among the seven lampstands. These are the seven congregations that represent the church of all ages. Especially for the church, which is living in the last minutes of the last hour, it is vital that we know Him.

Jesus deserves more than a nominal Church; rather, he deserves passionate followers who desire to change the world around them and understand that heaven's power and authority can only be released from a deep relationship with Him.

It is so good that you are making the decision to start a new habit; one that will become a new lifestyle for you, causing your prayer life to never be the same again.

So let's persevere and not give up, and call upon 'The Holy Spirit' to keep us motivated and full of desire to come face to face with the 'Christ of Heaven.' There is so much more to be revealed, and we are praying that this book will help you on your pathway of discovery.

At the end of each chapter, you will find a reflection by others that we have invited to share their understanding and revelations. Some will be well known to you, and others may not, but the important thing is that they too are on this same journey of discovery.

That a powerful unity may become visible between Jesus as the Head and us as His Body. We believe that two things are very important at this time:
1. To understand the original purpose of His church (Ekklesia).
2. To know Jesus as the Head of this church (Col. 1:18), while we are the Body (1 Cor. 12:13).

He longs for the cooperation between Himself as the Head and us as the Body. This will demonstrate to the world what a loving and powerful God He is. Together, we can discover and even rediscover the things that will bring us, as His Body, into complete unity with Him as the Head, so that His glory can be revealed to all of creation.

> *Our focus must be on getting to know Him better and understanding the original purpose of His church (Ekklesia).*

Intimacy with God

'Intimacy with God' is birthed from a deep desire to know God completely and allow yourself, without fear or shame, to be fully known by Him - it's a two-way street, and nothing is hidden. Intimacy in any relationship grows and develops because both parties are dedicated to sacrificing time and undivided attention to each other, sharing their innermost thoughts, and being completely transparent.

Do we dare to let God come so close? Can God know you in such a way and fill your heart with Himself? As you share with Him, He is also willing to share Himself with you.

This intimacy can sometimes be a struggle. Who and what do I give my time, energy, and space to? What fills my heart? The battle I feel for my heart's affection is evident every day, making it sometimes almost impossible to maintain. One day, I can feel so close, as if I am sitting on His lap; the next day, He seems a million miles away. We all experience this struggle; however, as we persevere and not give up, we will achieve that which we desire, and He will become the 'Lover of our soul.'

Imagine a world without intimacy: everything grey, devoid of emotion, warmth, or connection. It would be a cold, hard world—no arms around you, no compliments, no compassion, no kisses or encouraging words. How would you feel in such a world? Intimacy was not invented by humans; it comes from God. Our Father God is full of warmth, love, feeling, and emotion. He created us in His image to be like Him with the same emotional capacity. God knew that we would always fall short when measured up against Him; nevertheless, God, the creator of all things, felt it was worth it. We will always receive more than we are able to give and I suspect that as we make the move towards Him, God Himself is the one who is covering the greater distance.

Draw near to God and He will draw near to you...(James 4:8)

We know that the most perfect example of unity that presently exists is not found here on earth among humanity but divine, in heaven between the Father, Son, and Holy Spirit. Their relationship is perfect at all levels, as is their cooperation with each other regarding their common purpose and passion. Simply put, there is never a moment when the Godhead are not in perfect unity.

It's challenging to imagine such perfect unity existing in our broken world, but by observing the Trinity, we can begin to grow and obtain a clearer revelation. As we begin to realize that the Father, Son, and Holy Spirit share their most intimate thoughts with each other, this becomes an example for us to do the same. When we share our thoughts and feelings with our Heavenly Father, something incredible begins to develop: a satisfaction of the soul is established, and a conclusion is reached that we have been truly created for intimacy.

Living out this close relationship with God is only possible because of what Jesus accomplished on the cross. Jesus restored our connection with God; knowing Jesus means knowing God, which is why, throughout this book, the focus is on Him – 'The Magnificent Jesus.'

Therefore, I encourage you to be united in love and to attain the full riches of a complete understanding, to know the mystery of God, namely Christ, in whom all the treasures of wisdom and knowledge are hidden. For in Him dwells all the fullness of the Godhead bodily, and because you are united with Him, the head of all principalities and powers, you too are filled with His fullness (Colossians 2:2-3, 9-10).

> *.......that their hearts may be encouraged, being knit together*
> *in love, and attaining to all riches of the full assurance of*
> *understanding, to the knowledge of the mystery of God, both of*
> *the Father and of Christ, in whom are hidden all the treasures*
> *of wisdom and knowledge.*
> *(Colossians 2:2-3)*

The role of the inner room

When it comes to our relationship with Jesus, the relationship is no different from any other; its success will be determined by how much we are willing to invest. What has helped many, in addition to making time, is to have an inner room.

In the natural world, when creating intimacy with your partner, you look for a place where you will not be seen or disturbed. There, you can get to know the deepest and most intimate things about each other. Likewise, you deepen your relationship with God by spending time together in a hidden place or the inner room.

*But you, when you pray, go into your room, and when you have
shut your door, pray to your Father who is in the secret place;
and your Father who sees in secret will reward you openly.*
(Matthew 6:6 - NKJV)

Do you have an inner room where you can be together with the Father? What does that look like? Have you ever wondered if the Father would like to be in the same room with you? Did Jesus have an inner room? Where and when did He spend time with the Father?

The Greek word for the hidden or the inner chamber is the word 'Tameion.' At that time, this word was used for the room where you put something away or locked it up. Many houses had small cubicles where it was cool, a pantry that the owner had access to. This room could be locked and invisible from the outside; no one could see you there. Try to find your own personal 'Tameion,' a place where it is quiet and where no one sees you, only God. A place where there are no distractions and where you can focus completely on God. For Jesus himself, this was often on a mountain, in a secluded place away from His disciples, and sometimes even during the night.

We believe that the three main requirements needed for your inner room are solitude, silence, and no distraction.

Solitude because it's about God and you alone. We are all guilty of behaving differently when others are watching. In solitude, it allows us to be ourselves and do things for God and ourselves.

Silence makes you confront your real self. Your innermost thoughts and feelings surface, and the only voices to be heard in this silent space are your own and God's voice.

Focus because we live in a world that is shouting for our attention and demanding a response. Our priority in the 'inner room' is to be with God and to gaze upon the Lord. It is a time to shut out the distractions of the world around us. It's amazing, isn't it, to think that when we do these things and prepare the 'inner room,' the Father is already there, waiting for us. It suggests that he really likes that place, and it's worth the effort.

> *But you, when you pray, go into your (inner) room, and when you have shut your door,* ***pray to your Father who is in the secret place;*** *(Matthew 6:6)*

Now that I have made preparations, what now?

Honesty
God does not seek perfect words or a perfect character, but He does require exclusive access to our hearts. God is looking for an attitude of dependence, an acceptance that we cannot do anything outside of Him, which will give Him the space to do what He wants and needs to do.

Safety

You are safe in the inner room. We are all attacked from time to time, but the 'inner room' provides us with a safe place, a place where we are exposed to the truth. It's the God-truth that will set us free from fear and doubt.

God's Word

An important part of your time with God is reading and studying the Bible. Read it not only as knowledge but also as a letter to you. It is faith-building and life itself. Pray God's Word back to Him, and let it set you free.

Place, proclamation, promise, and power

When Jesus said, "On this rock I will build my 'Ekklesia,' and the gates of Hades will not overcome it" (Matthew 16 v 18), why did He use the specific Greek word 'Ekklesia?' Those listening would have needed no explanation as what it meant, unlike the people of today, who have been exposed to the translation of the King James writers. The instruction from their Sovereign was to use the word church and cancel the word ekklesia. This actually happened in the New Testament 115 times. It meant that often it carried with it a connection to a building and auto-cratic authority.

Currently, we believe that the Holy Spirit is focused on bringing us back to the original meaning and blowing away the fog that surrounds Ekklesia. It means assembly or gathering for a specific purpose. In Greek and later Roman times, its purpose was governmental as it made decisions about public affairs. Jesus best expressed the heavenly governmental purpose of His Ekklesia when He taught us to pray to His Father: "Your kingdom come, Your will be done on earth as it is in heaven."

The Ekklesia, as it gathers, can be open to discovering the governmental will of the Father through worship, teaching, breaking of bread, and prayers (Acts 2:42). It could also gather for a specific assignment—Matthew 18:15-20 describes a gathering of two or three to discover God's will around a topic. It is likely that the name Ekklesia is given to a combination of small and larger meetings. In the early church, they initially met in temples and houses, and later, they added larger buildings as they became available. However small or large our Ekklesia may be, it is scattered so that it can be 'apostled'—sent out into every sphere of society, to be the carriers of Kingdom culture and the channel through which Jesus disciples and transforms nations.

> *When Jesus came into the region of Caesarea Philippi, He asked His disciples, saying, "Who do men say that I, the Son of Man, am?" So they said, "Some say John the Baptist, some Elijah, and others Jeremiah or one of the prophets." He said to them, "But who do you say that I am?" Simon Peter answered and said, "You are the Christ, the Son of the living God."*
> *Jesus answered and said to him, "Blessed are you, Simon Bar-Jonah, for flesh and blood has not revealed this to you, but My Father who is in heaven. And I also say to you that you are Peter, and on this rock I will build My church, and the gates of Hades shall not prevail against it. And I will give you the keys of the kingdom of heaven, and whatever you bind on earth will be bound in heaven, and whatever you loose on earth will be loosed in heaven."*
> *Then He commanded His disciples that they should tell no one that He was Jesus the Christ.*
> *(Matt 16:13-20)*

I don't know how many times I have read or heard other people quote this portion of scripture during my lifetime. I guess it must have numbered in the hundreds, and possibly even in the thousands. Many others and I are familiar with this event at Caesarea Philippi. Yet, it is only recently that I have come to the realization of how inaccurate some of the interpretations have been, which has led to a false narrative and practice of how we do church. Therefore, it is vital that we understand what was really happening at Caesarea Philippi, the significance of Peter's revelation and the promise of Christ, as well as the impartation of power and authority received by the disciples.

- PLACE
- PROCLAMATION
- PROMISE
- POWER

The Place - Caesarea Philippi (City of Pagans)

Caesarea Philippi was situated near the foot of Mount Hermon and was a city known for its immoral activities and the worship of numerous demigods. To the pagan worshipping people who lived there, the cave at Caesarea Philippi created in their minds the belief that it was a gate to the underworld, where fertility gods lived – the gates of Hades.

As a result, they committed detestable acts of worship to these false gods and engaged in horrible deeds, including prostitution and sexual interaction between humans and animals. It was literally the darkest spiritual region in Palestine, and yet it was to this place that Jesus, for over eight hours on foot, journeyed with His disciples.

When the disciples arrived at this area, they must have been shocked. It must have been like the Lord had brought them to hell on earth, a place that every respectful Jew would have shunned and most certainly would avoid contact with the people of Caesarea Philippi.

During Old Testament times, this region of Israel became a centre for Baal worship, which eventually was replaced with the worship of Greek fertility gods. On the cliff above the city, local people built shrines and temples to Pan, which demonstrates how significant this specific area was. Satan had established himself here for thousands of years, and it was very deliberate that Jesus chose this place to confront the core beliefs of His disciples in relation to who He was thus presenting a clear challenge. Quite simply, He didn't want His followers hiding or ignoring whatever evil was around them; instead, He wanted them to confront it and storm the very gates of hell.

The Proclamation – You are the Christ

Standing near the pagan temples of Caesarea Philippi, Jesus asked His disciples, "Who do you say that I am?" Peter boldly replied, "You are the Christ, the Son of the living God."

Jesus continued, "You are Peter, and on this rock I will build my church, and the gates of Hades will not overcome it" (Matt. 16:13-20).

Though Christian traditions debate the theological meaning of those words, it seems clear that Jesus's words also had symbolic meaning. His church would be built on the "rock" of Caesarea Philippi, a rock literally filled with niches for pagan idols, where ungodly and evil values dominated.

Gates were defensive structures in the ancient world. By saying that the gates of hell would not overcome, Jesus suggested that those gates needed to be attacked. The disciples may have been overwhelmed by Jesus's challenge; they had, for instance, studied under their Rabbi for several years, and now He was commissioning them to a huge task: to attack evil and build the church in places filled with moral corruption.

The Promise – I will build my church

Jesus presented a clear challenge with his words at Caesarea Philippi: He didn't want his followers to hide from evil. He wanted them to confront it. By using the keys of the kingdom of heaven to bind on earth and loose in heaven, they would be able to contend in the heavens and, quite simply, establish His Ekklesia and bring heaven to earth.

Christ's mission is not to avoid the sinful culture around us but to confront it head-on. Many Christians have been taught to go on the defensive by shutting the door on the world around them, hiding and separating themselves and their homes from any perceived evil influences. This is the polar opposite of the assignment given to the church by Christ, who is the head of all principality and power, and has made us alive with Him, raised us up, and made us sit together in heavenly places in Christ Jesus.

The Power – Bind and Loose

In order to fulfil the mission of producing an unstoppable church, Jesus gave His disciples power and authority.

"And I will give you the keys of the kingdom of heaven, and whatever you bind on earth will be bound in heaven, and whatever you loose on earth will be loosed in heaven."
(Matthew 16:19)

This signifies a delegation of authority. In essence, Jesus is giving Peter, the other disciples, and the church as a whole the authority to make decisions or proclamations regarding matters of faith in relation to establishing His Kingdom here on earth just as it is in heaven.

You may, however, be asking the question – "What does this actually mean"?

We believe and understand that the 'Kingdom of God' is the spiritual realm where God's will is fully realised, and God's authority and rule are established. It represents a state of righteousness, peace, and justice and is to be established wherever life happens, not only among believers but also in every sphere of society. It's also both a present spiritual reality and a future eschatological fulfilment when Christ will reign on Earth for a thousand years, establishing peace and justice.

Purpose

The book that you have in your hand is an attempt to bring in-part a revelation as to who 'The Christ of Heaven' is. It would be futile to try to document anything other than a mere glimpse of what Christ in all of His glory might look like.

The apostle Paul knew how far away we are as mortal beings from receiving the full revelation, which is why he wrote......

*"For now we see in a mirror, dimly, but then face to face. Now I
know in part, but then I shall know just as I also am known".
(1 Corinthians 13:12)*

On this side of eternity, we will always fall short of fully understanding the splendour of who He really is.....

*"Eye has not seen, nor ear heard, nor have entered into the heart of
man, the things which God has prepared for those who love Him."
(1 Corinthians 2:9)*

We are convinced that it is the Lord's desire to reveal Himself to us, and consequently, it should be the pursuit of our hearts to receive as much of the revelation of Christ as possible.

"I want to know Him." In knowing Him, I shall become like Him, and I will become consumed with His love and live my life by His faith. I will also be fully equipped to fulfil His mission here on earth, but this can only be possible as more and more of Christ is revealed to me at a personal level. It is why John wrote...

*"Beloved, now we are children of God; and it has not yet
been revealed what we shall be, but we know that when He is
revealed, we shall be like Him, for we shall see Him as He is."
(1 John 3:2)*

Even though it will take the whole of eternity for Christ to be fully revealed, it is worth beginning that journey today, and it is our hope and prayer that this book will aid you in your quest, which is...

TO KNOW THE CHRIST OF HEAVEN.

About the prayer tool A.R.K.

There are various prayer tools you can use to deepen your encounter with Jesus. We have chosen the A.R.K. prayer tool because of our positive experiences with it. This tool has enriched our prayer life, guiding us in our conversations with Jesus and helping us build a closer relationship with Him.

It is important to cherish these moments of prayer and reflection. They give us the opportunity to pause, listen to His voice, and open our hearts to His guidance, allowing us to grow in our relationship with Him. At the end of each chapter, you will find a page for your own notes. We have included the A.R.K. questions at the top of that page, which you can use as a foundation. It involves three interactions:

A - Agreement stands for agreeing with who Jesus is; in essence, aligning with His testimony. We begin by agreeing with His identity. It's straightforward. For example, when Jesus declares Himself as the faithful witness (Revelation 1:5): "You are the Faithful Witness; You are the Firstborn from the dead. You are the Ruler of the kings of the earth. I agree with You; I declare it in Your presence." Declare His identity after each chapter. This act is at the heart of worship, aligning with who He is. Around the throne, they proclaim, "You are holy; You are good; You are worthy." They affirm with agreement who God is.

R - Revelation. We seek further revelation from the Holy Spirit. After agreeing, we pursue revelation. We pray: "Lord, reveal Yourself to me as the Faithful Witness. Tell me more about Yourself. Unveil more of who You are to me." Beloved, if you persistently ask Him, He will disclose more about Himself in this manner. Anything you persistently pray for in faith within God's will, you will receive. We ask Him for the revelation of Himself.

K - Keep it. We uphold the prophecy by responding in a specific way, in faith and obedience, to the truths He reveals in each description. We respond by committing ourselves. We declare: "I commit myself to obey You and to believe You in these ways." We commit to obedience in precise ways. We also seek Jesus' assistance. For instance, when we affirm, "You are a faithful witness," we declare it with agreement and then pray, "Lord, reveal Yourself to me in this way." Then we affirm, "Lord, I commit myself by the power of the Holy Spirit to be faithful and to stand for the truth regardless of the cost. Help me, Holy Spirit." We dedicate ourselves and ask for His help.

Song 'The Magnificent Jesus'

We are very pleased to announce that Luke Finch has composed an exclusive song titled 'The Magnificent Jesus' specifically for this book.

Before you start the next chapters, we invite you to watch and listen to this beautiful song.

Please scan the QR code.

Luke Finch

Photos in this book

In this book, we have included stunning photos that uniquely and powerfully capture each characteristic of Jesus. These images were carefully selected not only to illustrate His virtues but also to evoke deep reflection and inspiration. Take a moment to let each photo speak to you, allowing its message to resonate and draw you closer to understanding the profound nature of Jesus. Each image tells its own story and offers a fresh perspective on the qualities that define Him.

Though the photos in this book are presented in black and white, we wanted to give you the opportunity to experience them in their full, vibrant beauty. The contrast of light and shadow in the printed version brings out a classic elegance, but for those who wish to see the richness of the colours, we've added a QR code. By scanning it, you'll be able to explore the full-colour versions of these captivating images on our website: **www.themagnificentjesus.com**

There, the colours bring an added depth, revealing even more of the detail and emotion captured in each shot. Whether you view them in black and white or in colour, these photos are meant to inspire, uplift, and deepen your connection to the extraordinary character of Jesus.

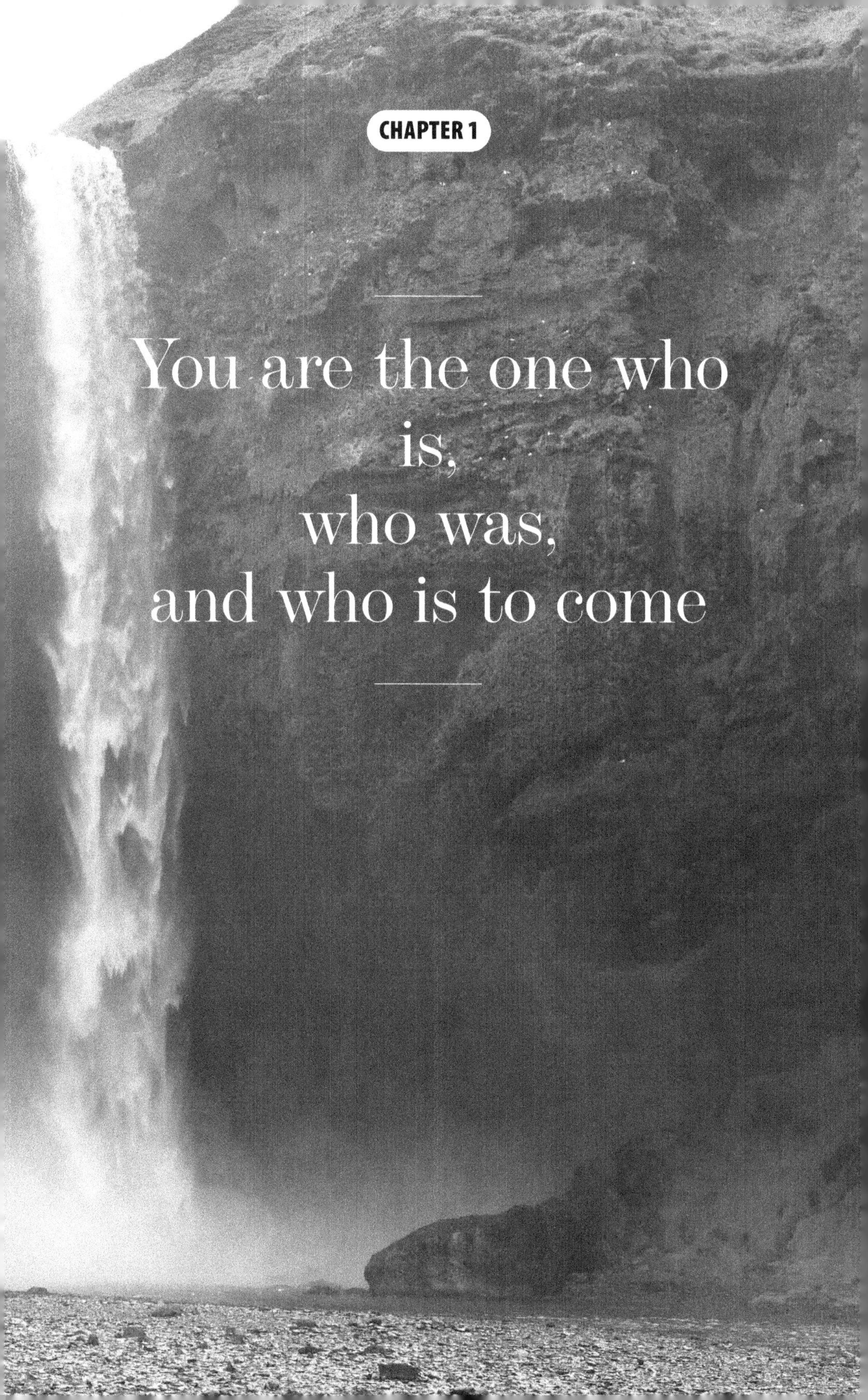

CHAPTER 1

You are the one who is,
who was,
and who is to come

"
Lord Jesus,
you are
unfathomable.
"

Prayer

Father in Heaven, we want to know You. Your son Jesus said, "He who has seen me has seen the Father" (Jn 14:9), so we make this conscious decision to press into Your Son. We want to know Him as the 'Christ of Heaven' – '**The Magnificent Jesus**' and, in so doing, comprehend who He really is. We ask that as we begin this journey and as the eyes of our hearts are opened, we will receive new insights and revelations that will change us forever.

> *The Revelation of Jesus Christ, which God gave Him to show His servants—things which must shortly take place. And He sent and signified it by His angel to His servant John, who bore witness to the word of God, and to the testimony of Jesus Christ, to all things that he saw. Blessed is he who reads and those who hear the words of this prophecy, and keep those things which are written in it; for the time is near.*
> *(Rev 1:1-3)*

In verse 4, we read: *Grace and peace to you from Him who is, who was, and who is to come.* What an incredible description of Jesus, which makes Him unique and distinct, above and beyond those in the heavens and those on earth, there is simply no-one like HIM.

You can only give what you already have, and Jesus has an abundance of Grace and Peace to bestow upon us. The incredible thing is that it has been our portion in times past; it is for this present day and will be there when we need it in the future and throughout eternity.

In relation to His eternal existence, 'The Message' translation puts it like this: THE GOD WHO IS, THE GOD WHO WAS, AND THE GOD ABOUT TO ARRIVE (MSG).

Jesus is present right where you are in this moment, just as He was in your past, which makes it a certain fact that He will always be in your future. It is actually impossible for Him to be anywhere or anything else. He was in the beginning, and in Him, there is no end. It's extraordinary, magnificent, amazing, astonishing.... the list goes on, but the truth is - He is indescribable.

Our prayer for today is that we surrender completely to this eternal God and ask God's Spirit for insights to better understand **The Magnificent Jesus**. According to this scripture, this blessing comes to us as we read the prophecy concerning Jesus aloud, not only to ourselves but also to the assembly. Look how the Amplified translates verse 3:

> *Blessed is the man who reads aloud the word of this prophecy; and blessed are those who hear [it read] and who keep themselves true to the things which are written in it [heeding them and laying them to heart], for the time [for them to be fulfilled] is near.*
> *(Revelation 1:3 Amp)*

King David also knew this pathway to blessing when he wrote:

> *Blessed is the man*
> *Who walks not in the counsel of the ungodly,*
> *Nor stands in the path of sinners,*
> *Nor sits in the seat of the scornful;*
> *But his delight is in the law of the LORD,*
> *And in His law he meditates day and night.*
> *(Ps 1:1-2)*

Reflection notes by Sarah-Jane Biggart

Lord Jesus, you are unfathomable. Who can fully comprehend the breadth of who you are? The God who existed before creation was spoken into being; the one who was with the Father *'in the glory you had before the world began'* (John 17:5). The God who was and is with us as 'Immanuel' (Matt 1:23). You, the one still yet to return and come again.

> *He who testifies to these things says, "Surely I am coming quickly."*
> *Amen. Even so, come, Lord Jesus!*
> *(Revelation 22:20)*

We are in awe of who You are, Jesus! The eternal, everlasting God! Who You are seems too much for us to grasp and beyond our human capacity. Please help us comprehend, Lord. Give us more understanding, we pray. Grant us access to deeper levels of Your spirit-taught wisdom at this time so that we might know You more completely. (See 1 Corinthians 2:6-15)

> *....that the God of our Lord Jesus Christ, the Father of glory, may*
> *give to you the spirit of wisdom and revelation in the knowledge of*
> *Him, the eyes of your understanding being enlightened; that you*
> *may know what is the hope of His calling, what are the riches of*
> *the glory of His inheritance in the saints, and what is the exceeding*
> *greatness of His power toward us who believe, according to the*
> *working of His mighty power.*
> *(Ephesians 1:17-19)*

> *The king answered Daniel, and said, "Truly your God is the*
> *God of gods, the Lord of kings, and a revealer of secrets, since*
> *you could reveal this secret."*
> *(Daniel 2:47)*

We say from the depths of who we are in this moment, for all our lives, day by day; we want to know you, Jesus, as the one who is from the beginning and as the one who remains King of all until the very end. We long to know you Lord, as the everlasting God who spoke the story of humankind from before the World existed, to be familiar with you, the one who holds all things created, seen, and unseen together. We desire to know you fully as Jesus Christ, as the one in your glory before creation and the one who reigns victorious, returning for His Bride at the time of the judgment of the living and the dead. We long to truly know you, Jesus. Father, we pray to reveal the fullness of the Son and His glory to us, the completeness of His glory today—His glory before creation and the glory yet to be revealed when He returns. We long to see you rightly and fully, Jesus Christ; in all, you are the Lord of all time.
Amen.

We are those alive today, hungry and searching to know Jesus Christ and His ways much more. As we determine our hearts to be open and hungry for greater intimacy with Him and knowledge of Him, it helps us to grasp that Jesus Christ, our Lord, is outside the restrictions of our human chronos time. He is the God who has been and will always be alive for all known time. Before our world's time even existed, He was and will be forever. He is not restricted by time, and in Him, neither are we.
He is beyond time, and yet He is fully accessible to us right now, today.
In this moment, Jesus longs to meet us where we are in our lives, here on earth, because He is our ever-present help. Yet, there is a dimension beyond the restrictions created by time in this world where we can meet Him as the God who is eternal.

Let us sharpen our focus on being with Him where He is now. In the place, 'beyond time' where He is longing to reveal Himself to us. Jesus, we long to be with you where you are in this moment. Eternal, everlasting Lord, what dimension of who you are would you like to reveal to us today? Please reveal yourself to us and speak to us, Lord, from that dimension. We long to understand more of who you are as the God who ever was and is.

 Walking in intimacy

Take a moment to consider this truth. The Son is the image of the invisible God, the firstborn of all creation. For in him, all things were created: things in heaven and on earth, visible and invisible, whether thrones or powers or rulers or authorities; all things have been created through him and for him.

> *He is the image of the invisible God, the firstborn over all creation.*
> *For by Him all things were created that are in heaven and that are*
> *on earth, visible and invisible, whether thrones or dominions or*
> *principalities or powers. All things were created through Him and*
> *for Him. And He is before all things, and in Him all things consist*
> *(Colossians 1:15-17)*

In Jesus Christ, our eternal God, all things hold together. What part of 'all things' is He longing to reveal to you at this moment? What aspects of Himself and how He operates is He inviting you to partner with Him as a co-labourer at this time?

According to the Word of God, there are times when He chooses to tell of things that no-one has yet heard or seen. Today is such a time.

From now on

> *I will tell you of new things of hidden things unknown to*
> *you. They are created now and not long ago; you have not*
> *heard of them before today.*
> *(Isaiah 48:6)*

Ask

What would you desire to reveal to me today of the hidden things, Lord? Wait on Him and receive. There is so much more of who He is and how we are to work with Him in these days to be revealed to us.

And now, O Father, glorify Me together with Yourself, with the glory which I had with You before the world was.. John 17:5

*"Very truly I tell you," Jesus answered, "before Abraham was
born, I am!"*
(John 8:58)

Word in the beginning

*In the beginning was the Word, and the Word was with God,
and the Word was God. He was in the beginning with God. All
things were made through Him, and without Him nothing was
made that was made. In Him was life, and the life was the light
of men. And the light shines in the darkness, and the darkness
did not comprehend it.*
(John 1:1-5)

Your Notes

Contemplate Jesus' characteristic highlighted in this chapter.
Note down your findings below.

- Agreement: Jesus, You are the one who is, and who was, and who is to come.
- Revelation: Lord, reveal Yourself to me as the one who is, who was, and who is to come. Tell me more about Yourself. Unveil more of who You are to me.
- Keep it: Lord, I commit myself by the power of the Holy Spirit to you. Help me, Holy Spirit. I dedicate myself and ask for your help. Overwhelm me by the fact that you are not restricted by time. You are beyond time, and you are fully accessible to us right now, today. You are always there!

CHAPTER 2

You have seven spirits before Your throne

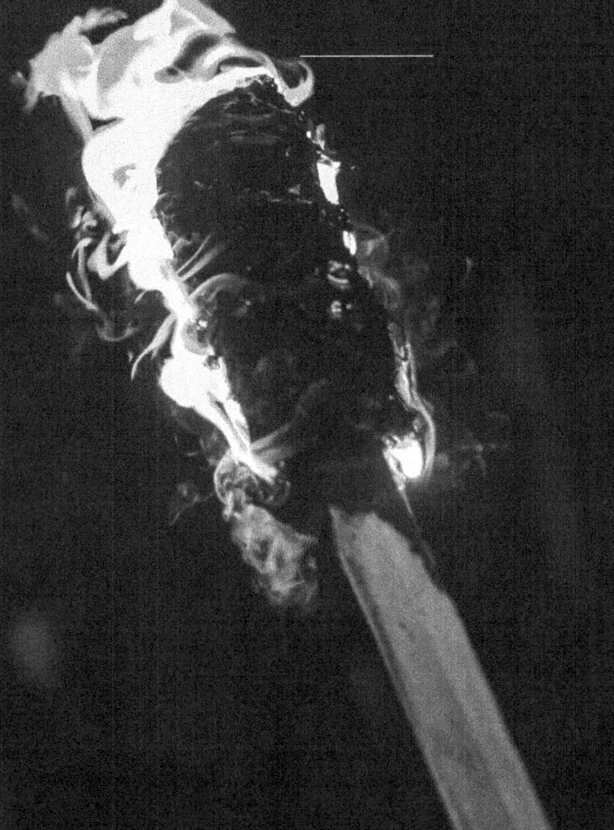

"

The Lord sees everything and knows everything.

"

Prayer: Lord, today, we pray that you will become our 'First Love' so that everything else fades into insignificance in the light of your glory and grace.

Jesus has seven spirits before His throne. In the book of Revelation, "these seven spirits" are mentioned three times. Listen to what the Word of God says.

These are the words of him who holds the seven spirits of God.
(Rev:3:1)

From the throne came flashes of lightning, rumblings and peals
of thunder. In front of the throne, seven lamps were blazing.
These are the seven spirits of God.
(Rev:4-5)

Then I saw a Lamb, looking as if it had been slain, standing at
the centre of the throne, encircled by the four living creatures and
the elders. The Lamb had seven horns and seven eyes, which are
the seven spirits of God sent out into all the earth.
(Rev 5:6)

John sees seven torches burning before the throne of God. and receives the revelation that these are the 'Seven Spirits of God.' The lamps represent the Holy Spirit's presence, which is often associated with fire. We know this because John warns some churches that the Holy Spirit can depart from them if they continue in their ways and do not change. Can you imagine a church without the Holy Spirit? Yet all across the earth, we can observe religious practice in the name of Christianity being performed without the presence of the Holy Spirit, and without the presence of the Holy Spirit, there is a real possibility for error and even sin both individually and at a communal level.

Look at the state of Israel (a type of the church) in the book of 1st Samuel. Eli is the priest, and his sons are out of control; because they don't know God, they no longer fear Him. They are literally robbing God of the offerings that the people are bringing to be sacrificed.
The son of Hannah, Samuel, is called to ministry at a young age, and God immediately speaks to him, saying that He is going to judge the nation of Israel—specifically Eli—because of their sin.

In 1 Samuel 4, Israel goes to war with the Philistines and are defeated, the Ark of the Covenant is captured, Eli's sons were both slaughtered, along with a great deal of the Israelite army, and Eli breaks his neck and dies. One of Eli's daughters-in-law was pregnant at the time of Israel's defeat and due to give birth. The news sent her into labour, and she gave birth to a son whom she called Ichabod, meaning the glory had departed. And truly, it had. The Ark of the Covenant – the dwelling place of God – had well and truly departed from Israel.

It is a serious place to find oneself, either individually or collectively, where the presence of the Lord is no longer manifested. It is on this very issue that Jesus calls the church the church at Ephesus to account.

This church is commended for its hard work and perseverance. They had even removed several false Christians and prophets from their assembly and endured much persecution for Christ's sake. They vehemently hated the acts of a false group known as Nicolaitians, but they were still not perfect. They had forsaken their first love because they were so occupied with performing their religious duties that they forgot the main purpose of their existence.

"Nevertheless, I have this against you, that you have left your first love. Remember therefore from where you have fallen; repent and do the first works, or else I will come to you quickly and remove your lampstand from its place—unless you repent".
(Rev 2:4)

The primary purpose for our existence is to worship Him before anyone or anything else, which means when I stand before Him at the end of time, He will only have one question for me: "How much did you love me?"

Let us approach Him today as our 'First Love'.

Reflection Notes by Wes Hall

The Lord sees everything and knows everything. The Spirit of God is pictured before the throne of God in Revelation Chapter 4 as seven lamps of fire that burn day and night. Lamps give light and illuminate the darkness. The lamp of fire in Bible times was used for bringing light into darkness. It was also used to uncover things that were hidden. Therefore, the symbol of a lamp in the Bible represents light, wisdom, and knowledge. The number seven represents perfection.

The Spirit of God is pictured as seven lamps and described as seven spirits, representing to us the fullness and perfection of wisdom, knowledge, and understanding that God possesses. In Revelation 5, the lamb is described as having seven eyes, which also depicts the fullness of the spirit of wisdom and knowledge possessed by Jesus, who is full of the Spirit of God.

Moses was commanded to place a lampstand with seven lamps of fire (Menorah) in the Holy Place before the Ark of the Covenant as a picture and reminder of the light and understanding that comes from the presence of the Lord. We serve a God who, by His Spirit, sees and knows everything and possesses perfect understanding and wisdom. By His wisdom and knowledge, He sustains all His creation.

In His perfect knowledge, nothing escapes His attention. He is the King of all kings and possesses perfect knowledge, understanding, and illumination of what is happening on earth. Nothing escapes His attention. His eye sees all: every righteous act and every unrighteous work. The Bible tells us that although the Spirit burns as seven lamps before God's throne, the eyes (or Spirit) of the Lord roam to and fro throughout the earth to show Himself strong on behalf of those whose hearts are loyal to Him.

Sometimes, in the midst of the chaos and difficulty on Earth, it is tempting to wonder whether God is aware of the injustice and unrighteousness that is taking place around us. Does God see? Does He understand? Does He have a plan or know what to do? As we meditate on the seven spirits of God, we are reminded that God sees all, understands all, and has a perfect plan to reward the righteous and deal righteously with all injustice and wickedness. By His sevenfold Spirit, He is gathering intelligence about every act of injustice and unrighteousness performed against His people, and He will grant speedy justice.

Though, from our perspective, God may seem to be silent and His intervention in the affairs of men delayed, He will answer from Heaven.

The Bible portrays our God and Saviour as the sovereign God seated on His throne. Yet, He is not a God who stands at a distance from the affairs of men. By His Spirit, He has perfect knowledge and understanding of the affairs of men. He knows what we know and also what we do not. He is in control of all things and, as the famous English preacher, John Wesley said, He is sitting on His throne, "ruling all things well."

Your Notes

Contemplate Jesus' characteristic highlighted in this chapter.
Note down your findings below.

- Agreement: Jesus, You have seven spirits before Your throne.
- Revelation: Lord, reveal Yourself to me as the one with seven spirits before Your throne. Tell me more about this. Unveil more of these spirits and your throne.
- Keep it: Lord, I commit myself to these seven spirits. Help me, Holy Spirit. I dedicate myself and ask for your help. Overwhelm me by these seven spirits. Show me your throne.

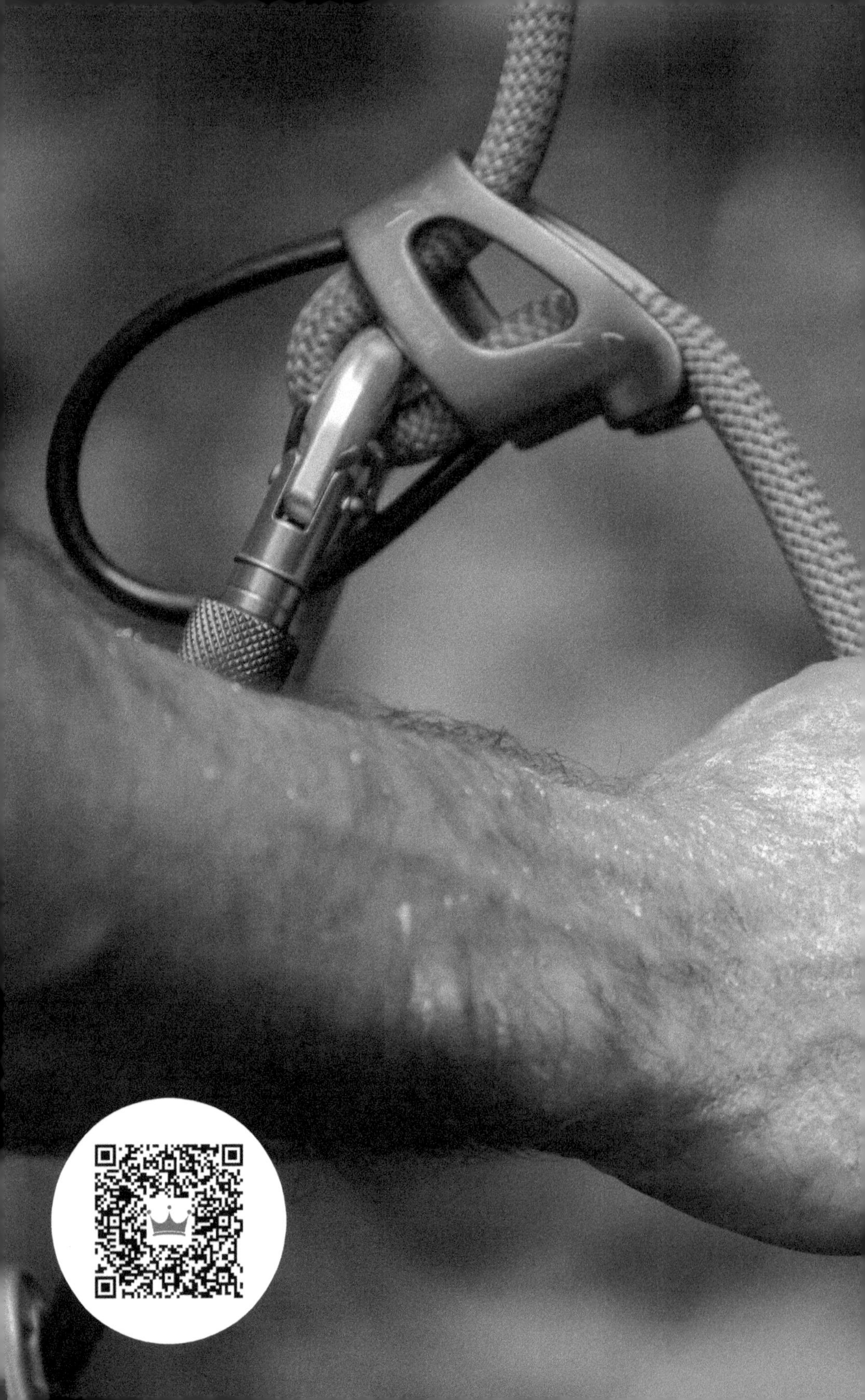

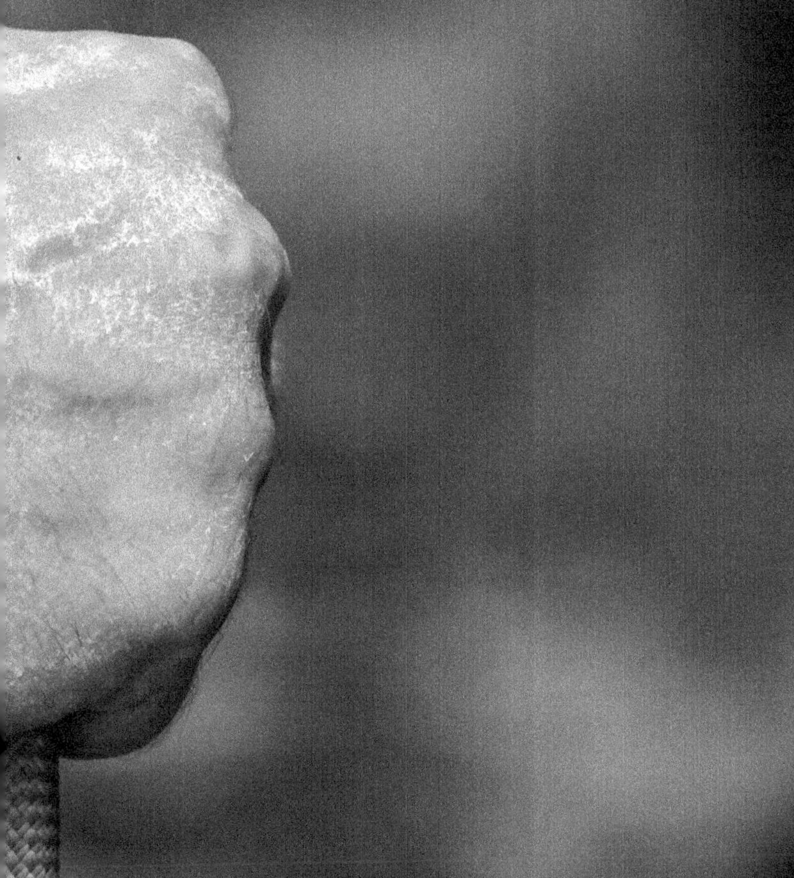

CHAPTER 3

You are the faithful witness

"

When Jesus
lived among
humanity,
he did so as a
perfect man...

"

Prayer: Our prayer today is that as we look upon the Lord, all doubt will be removed from our minds and hearts and that we will come to an assured understanding that in Christ is absolute truth.

An eyewitness in a court of law is one of the best types of evidence because an individual who personally observes an event, incident, or situation can provide first-hand testimony or information about what they saw. Prosecutors love this type of eyewitness testimony and consider it one of the most valuable in legal proceedings because it provides a direct account of events from those who were present. However, it's important to recognise that eyewitness testimony can be subject to biases, inaccuracies, and limitations due to factors such as perception, memory distortion, and external influences.

Jesus, on the other hand, has always been and will always be trustworthy. He was the ultimate faithful witness during His earthly ministry because it was impossible for Him to be anything else as He presented Himself as the embodiment of truth. He carried within Him an eyewitness account of all that had taken place even before creation and faithfully testified to His disciples and all of those within the sound of His voice. It left His hearers in no doubt that what they were hearing was the absolute truth from before the beginning of time. It gave them absolute confidence in His words, knowing that they could also be the same—faithful witnesses.

*Again, a new commandment I write to you, which thing is true
in Him and in you, because the darkness is passing away, and
the true light is already shining.
(1 Jn 2:8)*

From generation to generation, for over 2,000 years, the greatest story ever told has been passed on by faithful witnesses, men and women who have been persuaded and infected by the truth of His testimony.

As we stand before Him today, we also need to allow our hearts to be infected by His truth so that we can also be trustworthy enough to be the carriers of the story to our generation and beyond.

It's our desire today that you hear His voice among the many voices that demand to be heard, to listen for that gentle whisper leading me into all truth in order for me to become one of His Faithful Witnesses.

Reflection notes by Duncan Smith

When Jesus lived among humanity, He did so as a perfect man but was also 'Immanuel' – 'God with us', and because we know that it is impossible for God to lie, Jesus becomes the embodiment of truth. The title and term, "Faithful Witness", therefore underscores Jesus' absolute reliability and truthfulness. His testimony about God, about salvation, and about that which is yet to take place becomes absolute truth without error.

What a comforting truth it is to our souls to know that Jesus Christ holds the title 'Faithful Witness' (Revelation 1:5). We can only imagine how reassuring and encouraging this must have been for the first Apostles and early Christians as they endured persecution and even faced death, being able to call upon Jesus as the faithful witness. This truth would have been a constant reminder to them of Jesus' steadfastness and dependability in the face of their suffering.

It is so amazing that the Greek word for witness is martyrs; it's the root of the word martyr. Jesus' faithfulness is demonstrated through His willingness to suffer and die not just to redeem us from sin, but also to die for the TRUTH. His life and sacrificial death are the ultimate testimony to God's love, faithfulness, and justice.

Greater love has no one than this, than to lay down one's life
for his friends.
(John 15:13)

But God demonstrates His own love toward us, in that while we
were still sinners, Christ died for us.
(Romans 5:8)

This is why we, as believers, are encouraged to remain faithful even unto death.

*'They triumphed over him by the blood of the Lamb and by
the word of their testimony; they did not love their lives so
much as to shrink from death.'*
(Revelation 12:11)

I think of Stephen as he was being martyred; recorded in Acts 7, it says

*But he, full of the Holy Spirit, gazed into Heaven and saw the
glory of God and Jesus (as the 'Faithful Witness') standing at
the right hand of God. And he said, "Behold I see the Heavens
opened and the Son of Man standing at the right hand of God."*
(Acts 7:55-56)

Seeing the vision of Jesus, the Faithful Witness who gave His life for the
world but was resurrected three days after his crucifixion because He is the
Resurrection and the Life which empowered Stephen to face death with
great courage and love. Stephen cried out as they stoned him.

*"Lord Jesus, receive my spirit" and falling to his knees he cried
out with a loud voice, "Lord do not hold this sin against them."*
(Acts 7:59-60)

These words as he died as a faithful witness are almost identical to the words
of our Lord Jesus, the Faithful Witness who cried out on the Cross. Luke
23:34 says, "Father, forgive them for they know not what they do." and Luke
23:46 says, "Father, into Your hands I commit my spirit".
As a faithful witness, Jesus reveals the nature and character of God to humanity. He faithfully conveys God's will, love, and redemptive plan. Jesus'
role, then and now, is to make known the mysteries of God and the future
events that will unfold according to God's plan. It's a perfect plan testified
by a perfect witness, who serves as a model for Christian believers who, just
like Stephen, are called to emulate Jesus' faithfulness in their own witness,
standing firm in their faith amidst trials, persecution, and temptation.

One of the key elements of being a faithful witness is being filled and baptised with the Holy Spirit. Jesus Himself was filled with the Holy Spirit from birth and baptised in the Holy Spirit when the Holy Spirit descended upon Him at the river Jordan.

One of the first things He did when He was raised from the dead, Jesus said to the disciples, "Peace be with you, as the Father has sent Me, even so I am sending you." Then he breathed on them (verse 22) and said to them, "Receive the Holy Spirit!" (John 20:21)

Imagine what that moment must have been like for those apostles when the King of Glory breathed on them and said, "Receive the Holy Spirit?" I think they went flying backwards and fell to the ground, probably shaking violently!" The Holy Spirit came into them, and they were born again.

Yet Jesus tells the same apostles a few days later, as He's about to finally leave the Earth and ascend into Heaven, "You are witnesses of these things. And behold, I am sending the promise of my Father UPON you. But stay in the city until you are clothed with power from on high." Then he lifted his hands, blessed them, and ascended to Heaven right in front of their eyes.

They could have been thinking, "How come we have to wait in the city to be clothed with power? Didn't we receive the Holy Spirit when He breathed on us a few days ago? But that was the moment Jesus gave them the Holy Spirit IN them. The faithful witness of the Holy Spirit that Christ Jesus was now IN them the hope of Glory (Col 1:27). Now Jesus tells them to wait in Jerusalem for the Holy Spirit to come UPON them in power so that they can be faithful witnesses. Jesus repeats this to them in the first chapter of the Book of Acts.

Acts 1:5, Jesus says, "John baptised with water, but you will be baptised with the Holy Spirit not many days from now." Then, in verse 8, He says, "But you will receive power when the Holy Spirit has come UPON (capitalisation mine) you, and you will be My witnesses in Jerusalem and in all Judea and Samaria and to the end of the Earth."

Wow! This is amazing! Having filled His disciples with the Holy Spirit in them, the Faithful Witness Himself dwelling in them, then tells them that the same Holy Spirit that He himself is baptised with will come UPON them, and they will be faithful witnesses of the Faithful Witness to the world. I love this!

Ten days later, we know that these apostles, already filled with the Holy Spirit, suddenly heard the sound of a mighty rushing wind, and tongues of fire came into the room and rested on each of their heads. They spoke in new tongues and began behaving like men who looked drunk because they were baptised in the Holy Spirit and FIRE (Luke 3:16). People rushed from all over Jerusalem, Peter stood up and preached, and 3,000 people were saved (Acts 2). From that day forward, all the apostles became powerfully effective, faithful witnesses of the resurrection of Jesus Christ and were willing to give their lives as martyrs for His glory. History tells us that almost all of them were martyred.

In the very same way, each one of us must be born again. We are born of the Spirit. The Holy Spirit, the Spirit of God, dwells in us from that moment. (Romans 8:9) and we become one spirit with Jesus (1 Corinthians 6:17), receiving in us the Eternal Spirit, the Spirit of Christ dwelling in us and giving life to our mortal bodies. He is the Faithful Witness in us that we belong to Him. (Romans 8:9-11)

But, for us to be His faithful witnesses in the world, we also must be baptised with the same Holy Spirit. You can be baptised with the Holy Spirit! Wait upon the Lord until you are clothed with power from on high. Ask God to fill you with hunger and tenacity to ask for the Holy Spirit to come UPON you. Ask those who are baptised with the Holy Spirit if they will lay hands on you just like Paul did for the disciples he met when he first arrived in Ephesus (Acts 19:6).

When I was a student at university, I prayed fervently in secret that the Lord would give me a double portion of the anointing that He had given

Reinhard Bonnke, one of the greatest evangelists, who won 70 million people to Jesus through his preaching. He is with the Lord now. I asked the Lord if it would be a sign that He had answered my prayer if one day I met Reinhard Bonnke and he laid his hands on me and said those exact words.

Sure enough, 17 years later, my beloved pastor, John Arnott, asked Reinhard Bonnke in a car park in Toronto to lay his hands on me and give me the anointing on his life. Reinhard said' "It would be my pleasure!" I knelt before the great man, and he laid his hands on my head and prayed the Lord would give me anointing and declared, "I give you the double portion!" I was powerfully baptised in power and glory as God gave me the answer to my deepest longing. The Faithful Witness is so faithful! I know he can do the same for each of you who asks Him for the Holy Spirit upon you.

When we believe in Jesus, we can do all the things that Jesus Himself did in His Name and even greater things than He did because He has gone to the Father (John 14:12). So go for it! Be a faithful witness to the power of the Holy Spirit just like Stephen, Peter, and Paul, and all the mighty men and women throughout the ages since that first day of Pentecost.

Let's not forget that when standing before us as the Faithful Witness, Jesus also stands as King of Kings, Sovereign Ruler, and Judge of the World, titles that also highlight His absolute authority. His testimony, therefore, is not just reliable but also authoritative. As the Faithful Witness, He speaks with the authority of one who has seen and known God intimately.

Jesus' faithfulness is a key aspect of His victory over sin, death, and Satan. His faithful witness leads to His exaltation and the ultimate defeat of evil, and we are assured that through our own faithfulness, we can also share in His victory.

As we gaze upon Him today and look into His eyes, we are assured that our salvation is secure, that He loves us even when we sometimes don't love ourselves, and that we can believe everything that He says about us. He is the reliable and truthful revealer of God's will, the example of faithful suffering, and the authoritative figure who guarantees the ultimate victory of good over evil. This is why we call Him today 'The Magnificent Jesus.'

Your Notes

Contemplate Jesus' characteristic highlighted in this chapter.
Note down your findings below.

- Agreement: Jesus, You Are the Faithful Witness.
- Revelation: Lord, show me Yourself as the One who is the Faithful Witness. Tell me about Yourself.
- Keep it: Lord, I commit myself to be faithful. Help me, Holy Spirit. I dedicate myself and ask for your help.

CHAPTER 4

You are the first born from the dead

"

...Lord gave me the vision statement for my life...

"

........the firstborn from the dead
(Revelation 1:5)

Prayer: Lord, as we stand before you today, it is with hearts overflowing with gratitude for your willingness to die that we may become firstborn sons and daughters with yourself.

When Jesus conquered death, He didn't just obtain eternal life in heaven for us but also a blessed life here on earth. As the firstborn, He inherited everything that the Father possessed. He is the rightful heir and possessor of all that is required to live a victorious and purposeful life.

The bible informs us that we are joint heirs with Christ (Romans 8:17), which means that the inheritance given to Him by the Father is also mine. He is risen, He's alive, He is the firstborn, and as a result, he has created a whole new family tree with you and me as heirs of all that was promised.

There is coming a time when all of us will be like Him. He was the **first** to receive a resurrection body, and we will also rise from the dead and experience the same. He overcame death and was the first to cross the finish line, which allowed us to do the same.

Traditionally, the firstborn received the inheritance from his father (the birthright), and you remember that Jacob cheated his brother Esau out of this. As the firstborn, Esau was the legal successor of all that his father possessed but despised it by selling it to Jacob for a bowl of stew. We are joint heirs with Christ; therefore, there is no need for us to work in order to buy our birth-right. Jesus purchased it on our behalf, making us, with Him, the rightful heirs of the inheritance, and He did this by being the firstborn from the dead.

In the New Testament, Jesus is referred to as the 'firstborn,' being the 'first-born' over all creation, emphasising his pre-eminence and role in creation. Similarly, he is the 'firstborn' among many brothers and sisters, highlighting his status as the pre-eminent one among believers.

> *He is the image of the invisible God, the firstborn over all creation. For by Him all things were created that are in heaven and that are on earth, visible and invisible, whether thrones or dominions or principalities or powers. All things were created through Him and for Him. And He is before all things, and in Him all things consist. And He is the head of the body, the church, who is the beginning, the firstborn from the dead, that in all things He may have the pre-eminence.*
> *(Col 1:15-18)*

> *And we know that all things work together for good to those who love God, to those who are the called according to His purpose. For whom He foreknew, He also predestined to be conformed to the image of His Son, that He might be the firstborn among many brethren.*
> *(Rom 8:28-29)*

What an inheritance!

Reflection notes by Franklyn Spence

...the firstborn from the dead (Resurrection Power)

Years ago, the Lord gave me the vision statement for my life and ministry that I'd like to share with you. This continues to challenge me to step into the fullness of what God has for me:

> *"I refuse to live an ordinary Christian life when I serve and am filled with an extraordinary God."*

I feel that I would be doing Jesus an injustice by setting my sights on a target that is lower than what God has set for me. If I truly believe that the resurrected Christ fills me, then I am confronted by the fact that normal is no longer my portion in life and that I must do all that I can to align myself as a joint heir and live a supernatural life.

It begs the question of how, as a joint heir with Christ, do we live a supernatural resurrected life?

In Colossians 1:18, Paul also describes Jesus as "the firstborn from the dead."

> *And He is the head of the body, the church, who is the*
> *beginning, the firstborn from the dead, that in all things He*
> *may have the pre-eminence.*
> *(Colossians 1:18)*

This powerful image reminds us that Jesus didn't just come back to life – He conquered death itself. He is the very embodiment of the resurrection power of God! And the amazing truth is, He wants to share that victory with us!

By definition, you can't have a resurrection without there first being a death. I know that I am stating the obvious, but there is a need to clearly understand what it is and isn't. We are not, for instance, talking about 'Renewal' or 'Revival' because neither requires a death; only a resurrection requires something to die. As is often the case, God's incredible blessings are given to us in seed form, and every seed must die to spring into resurrected life and produce a harvest. So the question is, what in our lives needs to die so that the seeds of blessing that God has given you can be resurrected?

> *Most assuredly, I say to you, unless a grain of wheat falls*
> *into the ground and dies, it remains alone; but if it dies, it*
> *produces much grain.*
> *(John 12:24)*

It is worth noting that every seed planted by God contains resurrection life and will always be perfect. It suggests that if it is not producing the desired result, then something else is wrong, so could it be that the soil of your heart is not fertile enough? In scripture, we see how critical the condition of the soil is for the seed to germinate.

> *Then He spoke many things to them in parables, saying:*
> *"Behold, a Sower went out to sow.*
> *And as he sowed, some seed fell by the wayside ......*
> *Some fell on stony places.....*
> *And some fell among thorns....*
> *But others fell on good ground and yielded a crop: some a*
> *hundredfold, some sixty, some thirty.*
> *(Matthew 13:1-9)*

Maybe today, as you gaze upon Jesus – 'The firstborn from the dead' – you have to acknowledge that you are in a deserted place, and you can't see any way that the seeds God has given you could ever grow. The conditions aren't right, the soil is too poor, mountains and valleys surround you, and you and everyone around you seem like spiritual dry bones. In that place, the resurrection power of Jesus can seem far away, but it is not as far as it seems.

But if the Spirit of Him who raised Jesus from the dead dwells
in you, He who raised Christ from the dead will also give life to
your mortal bodies through His Spirit who dwells in you.
(Romans 8:11)

The journey to discover and ultimately experience this resurrection power is to remind yourself that your words have supernatural power when spoken in faith. You are able to declare and proclaim that because Jesus is resurrected, then you also, as a joint heir, can participate in that same power.

This charge I commit to you, son Timothy, according to the
prophecies previously made concerning you, that by them you
may wage the good warfare,....
(1 Tim 1:18)

Take time to remember and declare those words today, decree those words, and call those mountains to come down! The mountains in our lives must move when confronted by the word of the Lord.

Here, we begin to see the true power, as this resurrection power is starting to flow. Because we serve the risen and resurrected Jesus, the one who conquered death and rose again – the firstborn from the dead – his words in our mouth are infused with resurrection power and life.

Let that sink in for a moment – we're infused with new life, actually partnering with him in resurrection! He is not the last; He is the firstborn from the dead. He is opening the way for all who believe to enter. This resurrection power isn't just for the afterlife. It's for here and now. It's the power to overcome sin, break free from old habits, and live with joy and purpose. It's the power to become who God created you to be. But it's more than that. In becoming one with him in his death and resurrection, infused with the same power that raised Jesus from the dead, the same Holy Spirit, we actually have resurrection power to speak life!

It's our privilege to gaze upon the Lord and be amazed at His sacrificial death and resurrection while telling the dry bones to come to life – BE RESURRECTED!

Your Notes

Contemplate Jesus' characteristic highlighted in this chapter.
Note down your findings below.

- Agreement: Jesus you are the firstborn from the dead.
- Revelation: Jesus, Show me Your glory as the firstborn from the dead. Speak to me; talk to me.
- Keep it: Lord, I commit myself to you. Help me, Holy Spirit. I dedicate myself and ask for your help. Overwhelm me with your glory.

CHAPTER 5

You are the ruler of kings on the earth

"

...every king, president and prime minister ultimately bows their knee to Jesus.

"

Prayer: Lord, today we want to acknowledge You as the supreme ruler.

How incredible it is that Jesus should be given the title 'Ruler of the kings of the earth.' It simply means that every earthly monarch, ruler, president, CEO, celebrity, dictator, and so-called supreme leader will bow before Him and acknowledge Jesus as King of kings and Lord of lords.

Not only is He the highest authority on earth, but He is also supreme over all of the gods of the unseen world. Look at the realisation that dawned upon King Nebuchadnezzar in the time of Daniel.

> *...... The king answered Daniel, and said, "Truly your **God is the God** of gods, the Lord of kings, and a revealer of secrets".....*
> *(Dan 2:47)*

Today, we want to acknowledge Jesus as the rightful heir of the earth, as the King of kings Who will one day come again to reign over His Kingdom here on earth. As such, He has become our great hope today, and the only solution to all that we see is wrong in the world around us.

There is a time when all kingdoms will have no choice but to submit under His rule; look at what it says in Revelation.

The seventh angel sounded his trumpet, and there were loud voices in heaven, which said: "The kingdom of the world has become the kingdom of our Lord and of his Messiah, and he will reign for ever and ever." (Revelation 11:15)

Paul acknowledged the same when he wrote:

For it is written:
"As I live, says the LORD,
Every knee shall bow to Me,
And every tongue shall confess to God." (Rom 14:11)

Also, to the church, he wrote:

...He raised Him from the dead and seated Him at His right hand in the heavenly places, far above all principality and power and might and dominion, and every name that is named, not only in this age but also in that which is to come. And He put all things under His feet, and gave Him to be head over all things to the church, which is His body, the fullness of Him who fills all in all.
(Eph. 1:20-23)

As we stand before Him today, He becomes our righteous judge in all things, and because He has the final ruling, no 'Court of Appeal' or 'Supreme Court' can overrule. Jesus has and always will have the final word.

Finally, there is laid up for me the crown of righteousness, which the Lord, the righteous Judge, will give to me on that Day, and not to me only but also to all who have loved His appearing.
(2 Tim 4:8)

How can we be anything else but be amazed as we stand in awe of Jesus, the supreme ruler over everything that exists now and yet to come.

Reflection notes by Murray Hiebert

I'm staring at the traffic in both directions in front of my favourite coffee shop. I can't help but wonder if, at times, the flow of traffic inside my mind looks the same. Always a new thought, a new emotion. Some moments were filled with the greatest of joys and some with intolerable pain. I'm guessing that might be true for you too.

At times, it seems as though the traffic of hard things is busier, doesn't it? For some, it's just a lonely day, and we're looking for someone who can be a friend. Some are feeling stuck in the same cycle of sin. Some are facing terminal illness. For others, it's an ageing parent who seems to be slipping away. Teenagers are growing up and getting ready to leave home, and we're wondering if we did enough. The bills are due, there isn't enough money, and we've been behind for a while. There's division in your church, and it's affecting your friendships. Or perhaps the family couldn't get together for Christmas because of real pain we didn't know how to get past. I don't know what it is for you, but I do know the feeling. And I know pain so deep it feels like you're going to drown.

And that's just the stuff you're dealing with! It says nothing of the pain and crisis in the lives of your friends, family, co-workers, and neighbours. And then add all of that to the growing global unrest and economic crisis, and we have a real reason to live in a constant state of anxiety.

How do we survive? How do we make it through another day?

In Chapter One of Revelation, John begins writing to seven churches in the region. It's clear that every church is dealing with crises, turmoil, and persecution. So, John starts with a glimpse of the beauty of Jesus to reassure, encourage, strengthen, and bring hope to weary people. And the good news for all of us today is that this glimpse still holds the same power.

When everything around me is shaking, I can still bring my fears to the Ruler of the kings of the earth. It's a breathtaking thought but not something that many people really think about. Most often, we see Jesus as a nice guy who comforts us, heals us, or meets our needs, but we don't often think of him literally as the King over all kings and the Lord over all lords. When Jesus rose from the dead, he was exalted to the highest place and given a name that is above every name, and we're told that at the mention of his name every knee will bow. This is much more than a symbolic submission in our hearts. It literally means that every king, president and prime minister ultimately bows their knee to Jesus. The Bible tells us that God sets up kings, and he tears them down. Ultimately, He has crowned Jesus as King forever on His Holy mountain, and Jesus will rule every nation.

Think about it! The one who knows you best, loves you best, and leads you best is the ruler of all things. If I can lean into this truth, it can change everything about my perspective today. While the traffic in my mind is filled with trouble, and it feels like my world is shaking all around, Jesus is in control of the biggest events on the planet. And if He can bring all these things together for His good and His glory, surely He can lead my life to the same end. Surely, I can trust him with my mess. Surely, He is able to handle what concerns me today. Surely, I can have hope today. Surely, I can see with eyes of faith today. Surely, I can remain in Him today.

Friends, lean into Jesus! He is the Ruler of the kings on earth!

Your Notes

Contemplate Jesus' characteristic highlighted in this chapter.
Note down your findings below.

- Agreement: Jesus, You are the Ruler of the kings of the earth
- Revelation: Lord, reveal Yourself as the ruler of the earth. Tell me more about your power. Unveil more of your kingship.
- Keep it: Lord, I commit myself to your power. Help me, Holy Spirit. I dedicate myself and ask for your help. Overwhelm me with your strength.

CHAPTER 6

You love us

“

...a profound depiction of God's love...

”

But God demonstrates His own love toward us, in that while we were still sinners, Christ died for us.
(Rom 5:8)

Prayer: As I stand before you today, Lord, I want to thank You that while I was dead in my trespass and sin, you demonstrated Your love towards me by being willing to die an innocent death on my behalf. Today, I desire for the love of God to saturate every molecule of my being, causing me to demonstrate that same love to the world around me.

'Jesus, the lover' is probably the most familiar description of Jesus that is known to us all. He loves us today with an unconditional love, and He is not looking for a time when we become worthy of His love – He is not moved emotionally, nor is He saying, "If you love me, I will love you in return." It is simply that He has set His love upon us, which is a decision of His will.

His great love for us covers our sins, guilt, shame, and failings. It is the great constant in the universe. When everything else has passed away, the one thing that will still remain is Christ's love.

For I am persuaded that neither death nor life, nor angels nor princi-palities nor powers, nor things present nor things to come, nor height nor depth, nor any other created thing, shall be able to separate us from the love of God which is in Christ Jesus our Lord. (Rom 8:38-39)

Even though I mentioned earlier that Christ's love towards us is a decision of His will, it doesn't mean for one moment that He doesn't feel it at an emotional level. I believe that Christ is deeply in love with us and feels it emotionally as lovers would toward one another. Quite simply, He is actually in love with us.

My advice to you today is to read the Song of Solomon and let the words of 'The Beloved' minister to your soul as you realise that there is no greater lover in all of the universe.

You have ravished my heart, my sister, my spouse; you have ravished
my heart with one look of your eyes, with one link of your necklace.
(Songs 4:9)

As Jesus causes His face to shine upon you today, why don't you lift your head towards heaven and allow yourself to feel his love being poured out upon you in every part of your being.

And we are His portion, and He is our prize
Drawn to redemption by the grace in His eyes
If grace is an ocean, we're all sinking
So Heaven meets Earth like an unforeseen kiss
And my heart turns violently inside of my chest
I don't have time to maintain these regrets
When I think about the way He loves us

He loves us!

Reflection notes by Steve Uppal

The Transformative Power of God's Unconditional Love

The Bible gives a profound depiction of God's love for humanity. This love is a cornerstone of our Christian faith and can deeply transform our relationship with God, ourselves, and others. Here are some foundational aspects of God's love, each revealing a different dimension of its depth and power. Remember that these truths can empower and deepen one's relationship with God and, therefore, should be pondered and prayed to get the full revelation.

God loves us as a perfect Father loves His children. In 1 John 3:1, it is written, "See what great love the Father has lavished on us, that we should be called children of God! And that is what we are!" Every human has a father wound that only the Heavenly Father can heal. Each of us is created to know and to be known by God in an intimate, loving relationship. God's love for us is deeply relational. It heals, restores, gives confidence, and causes a person to flourish. Each of us is created to live in the experience of this love. God's love is not abstract or distant but personal and intimate. Psalm 139:1-2 highlights this beautifully: "You have searched me, Lord, and you know me. You know when I sit and when I rise, you perceive my thoughts from afar." God knows each of us individually and loves us uniquely. This personal attention means that God's love is tailored to our individual needs and circumstances.

God's love is unconditional. Unlike human love, which often depends on the behaviour or qualities of the person being loved, God's love is rooted in His own nature and character. The apostle Paul emphasises this in Romans 5:8: "But God demonstrates his own love for us in this: While we were still sinners, Christ died for us." God's love does not depend on our worthiness or merit; it is a gift that is freely given.

God's love is eternal. Jeremiah 31:3 declares, "I have loved you with an everlasting love; I have drawn you with unfailing kindness." This eternal aspect of God's love means that it is steadfast and unchanging, regardless of our circumstances. Unlike human love, which can waver and fade, God's love endures forever. We never have to wonder whether he is in a good mood or not.

God's love is sacrificial. The ultimate demonstration of God's love is seen in the sacrificial death of Jesus Christ. John 3:16, one of the most well-known verses in the Bible, states, "For God so loved the world that he gave his one and only Son, that whoever believes in him shall not perish but have eternal life." This sacrificial love is at the heart of our Christian gospel, showing that God's love involves personal cost and profound generosity.

God's love is perfect, with no ulterior motives or imperfections. 1 John 4:18 states, "There is no fear in love. But perfect love drives out fear, because fear has to do with punishment. The one who fears is not made perfect in love." God's perfect love seeks what is best for us, fostering trust and security, unlike human love, which can often be flawed and self-seeking. Therefore, we can trust him without question or fear.

God's love is transformative. 2 Corinthians 5:17 explains, "Therefore, if anyone is in Christ, the new creation has come: The old has gone, the new is here!" God's love has the power to change us from the inside out, enabling us to love others as He loves us. This transformation is reflected in our actions, attitudes, and relationships, making us more compassionate, forgiving, and selfless.

God's love is rooted in His nature. The Bible succinctly states that "God is love" (1 John 4:8). Love is not merely an attribute of God; it is fundamental to His very being. This means that all of God's actions are motivated by love, and His love is the source of all true love in the universe. Understanding this helps us trust God's intentions and plans for us, knowing that they are rooted in love.

God's love is unbreakable. Romans 8:38-39 provides a powerful assurance: "For I am convinced that neither death nor life, neither angels nor demons, neither the present nor the future, nor any powers... will be able to separate us from the love of God that is in Christ Jesus our Lord." This unbreakable bond means that nothing can sever the connection between God and those who trust in Him, offering immense comfort and stability.

God's love is a deliberate choice. Ephesians 1:4-5 reveals, "For he chose us in him before the creation of the world... In love, he predestined us for adoption to sonship through Jesus Christ, in accordance with his pleasure and will." God chooses to love us, not out of obligation but because it is His nature to do so. This choice underscores the freedom and grace inherent in divine love. As we grow in understanding by experiencing God's love, we are changed from within, becoming more like the One who loves us beyond measure. It empowers us to love others selflessly and sacrificially, reflecting the divine love we have received. The Holy Spirit helps us to know God as Father or Abba (Romans 8.15, therefore, I would encourage you to pray through the above points on God's love, asking the Holy Spirit to be the Spirit of Wisdom and Revelation, making these truths a reality.

Your Notes

Contemplate Jesus' characteristic highlighted in this chapter.
Note down your findings below.

- Agreement: Jesus, You love me.
- Revelation: Lord, reveal Yourself to me as the one who has really loved me. Let me feel it. Unveil more of your unconditional love.
- Keep it: Lord, I commit myself to your love. Help me, Holy Spirit. I dedicate myself and ask for your help. Overwhelm me with the love of Jesus. I love you!

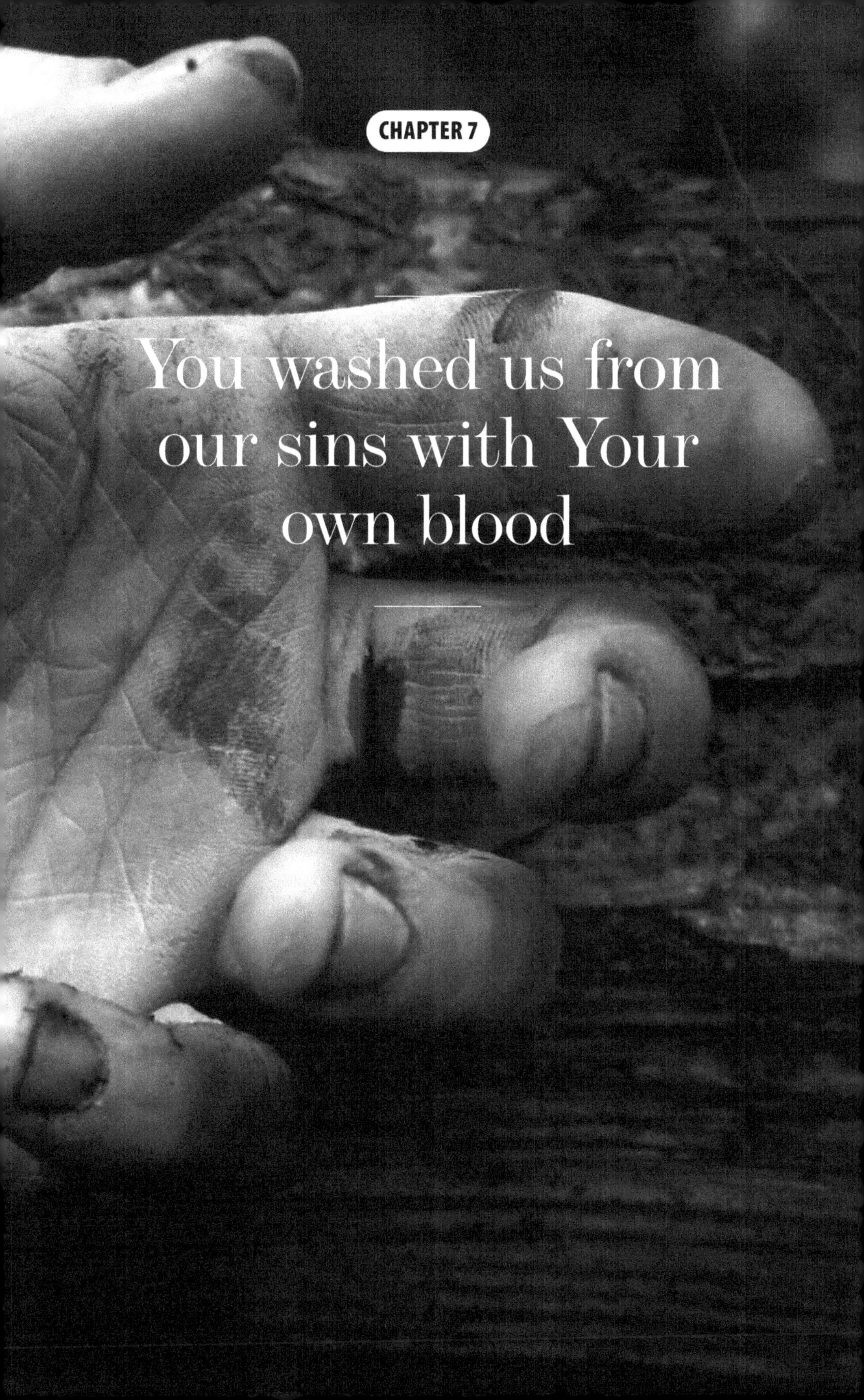

CHAPTER 7

You washed us from our sins with Your own blood

"

He is the
perfect
fulfilment of
God's perfect
justice.

"

...and has freed us from our sins by his blood
(Revelation 1:5)

Likewise, He also took the cup after supper, saying, "This cup is the new covenant in My blood, which is shed for you. (Luke 22:20)

Prayer: Today, Lord, I want to thank you that I can stand before you washed and my conscience cleansed because you, as my High Priest entered the Most Holy Place once and for all and shed every last drop of your precious blood.

When Jesus died on the cross, every last drop of His blood was poured out, not accidentally spilt but consciously shed! This was an act of His will and not the actions of those who believed they had the authority to take His life or save it. Only Jesus Himself had the authority to determine His fate. He could have summoned the hosts of heaven or simply decided not to endure the horrors of the cross, but He did neither; instead, He surrendered His will to the will of the Father.

He went a little farther and fell on His face, and prayed, saying, "O My Father, if it is possible, let this cup pass from Me; nevertheless, not as I will, but as You will." (Mat 26:39)

There is power in the shed blood of Jesus that doesn't exist in the blood of animals sacrificed in the old covenant, no matter how spotless that animal was. Animal blood merely provides a covering, whereas Christ's shed blood provides a cleansing.

His blood is also priceless; with it, He has bought us. There is no one besides Him who could have done this. Imagine if Jesus didn't exist; what if He hadn't gone on the cross? What a different world we would live in today. Our hearts would only experience evil, hurt, and despair, and as a result, we would live and die, having never experienced the goodness of God.

By going to the cross, Jesus became our saviour and obtained power and authority to cleanse and redeem us, liberate us, and heal us. No one else was perfect enough to do this.

In Him, we have redemption through his blood, the forgiveness of sins, in accordance with the riches of God's grace. (Eph. 1:7)

If we were to spend every second of every day for the rest of our lives thanking Him for what He has done, it wouldn't be enough. However, we have an invitation to reason with the Lord and talk to Him about our sins. He is willing and able (because of the shed blood) to completely remove every trace and stain of sin.

"Come now, and let us reason together, Says the LORD, Though your sins are like scarlet, They shall be as white as snow; Though they are red like crimson, They shall be as wool."
(Is 1:18)

Reflection notes by John Arnott

Why did Jesus have to die and shed his blood? Christians are aware that Jesus died for them, but why was that necessary? It has everything to do with the perfect justice of God. Are you glad that God is perfect? Really and truly? What are the implications for you? He requires that every injustice be put right, every wrong must be compensated for and repaid - put right. We notice throughout the Old Testament the importance of the sacrifice. It had to be without blemish and spot; why?

Adam and Eve, in the Garden of Eden, ate the forbidden fruit and are now hiding in guilt and shame. They are clothed in fig leaves, and God said, "Fig leaves are not adequate. And He made them clothes of skins. Why? Because an animal had to die, shed its blood, and surrender its skin to provide a proper covering? And God accepted that as an atonement or covering for their sin. So, we see the leading biblical characters sacrificing animals as a means of forgiveness and a covering for sin. Noah, Abraham, the patriarchs, etc., all practised this.

Let's consider Moses, who instituted the Passover, which we want to look at. The final plague of Egypt is about to happen. Moses is told, "Tell the people to sacrifice a perfect lamb, one-year-old, catch the blood in a basin, and then splash it onto the lentil and the two side posts of your house door. (Make the sign of the cross in blood) My judgement will pass through the land tonight, and when I see the blood, I will 'passover' you, and you will be spared and protected.

So Israel sacrificed from that day on, in the Tabernacle and later in Solomon's temple, to make atonement, a covering for sin.
Scripture tells us that Life is in the blood. And here we see the divine exchange. The innocent dies for the guilty, and the debt is paid by another who loves him. And the guilty one goes free when they repent and believe.

Hebrews 10:4 tells us, 'It is impossible for the blood of bulls and goats to take away sins,' ... but a body you prepared for me;

Jesus Christ – The Magnificent Jesus is that prepared offering for you and me.

When John the Baptist saw Jesus coming, he declared, "Look, the Lamb of God, who takes away the sin of the world."

In that phrase, the Prophetic type and mystery are revealed. So how does it work? It works because it is a Prophetic picture. A type and symbol that points to Jesus Christ, the lamb of God who will come and take away the sin of the world. He is the perfect fulfilment of God's perfect justice.

Consider Abraham and Isaac from Genesis Ch. 22:1-18.
I did not really understand this story for years. I realised God was testing Abraham, but I could never figure out why such a cruel test. An old man of perhaps 114 years is asked to take the life of his young son as a test of his obedience.God, what is this? It seems cruel and completely out of character for you until we realise that Abraham represents God, and Isaac is a type of Jesus, His Son. We see them going up the hill together, one of the mountains of Moriah, probably Mount Calvary. Isaac is carrying the wood on his back, just like Jesus. They build the altar together and put the wood on it. Isaac, possibly about 12 years old, complies and climbs on top of the altar, lying on the wood. Abraham is determined to do it, and as he is about to strike with the knife, the angel of the Lord says, "Stop, this was a test of your obedience." Then they find a ram caught in the thicket that is sacrificed instead of Isaac. A substitutionary death.

I asked the Lord with tears one day why He would do this to an old man and his beloved son. He said, "I wanted to know if there was a father anywhere who was willing to do what I am about to do with My Son." And Abraham was willing...

Jesus had to die, friends, and the perfect Son of God became the perfect sacrifice. Worth more than all of us put together, He traded His life for yours and mine and poured out His precious blood that cried for mercy; "Father, forgive them they know not what they do" Luke 23:34.

May the blood of Jesus cleanse you right now as you meditate on the fact that love was His motivation.

For God so loved the world that he gave his one and only Son, that whoever believes in him shall not perish but have eternal life. John 3:16

Your Notes

Contemplate Jesus' characteristic highlighted in this chapter.
Note down your findings below.

- Agreement: Jesus, You freed me from my sins by your blood
- Revelation: Lord, reveal Yourself to me as the one who freed me from my sin. Tell me more about the power of your blood. Unveil more secrets.
- Keep it: I commit myself fully to You, dedicating my life to walking in the protection, cleansing, and covering that Your blood provides each day. May I always remain aware of the transforming power of Your blood in my life.

CHAPTER 8

You are the maker of a kingdom and priests

> "...He is indeed the Magnificent King of all kings..."

Prayer: Holy Spirit of God, give us revelation today of what it really means for us to be a 'Royal Priesthood' and how we can be more effective in our governance of 'Christ's Kingdom' here on earth.

Jesus – The Christ of Heaven – is co-eternal with the Father and the Holy Spirit, through whom all things were made. This is not a fantasy born out of myth and legend but a reality rooted in scripture, which is the foundation of Christian faith and theology. Is it any wonder that, down through the ages, the devil has sought to attack this truth? For to accept that creation is the result of intelligent design is to accept the existence of God Himself.

However, it's important to note that perspectives on the origin and nature of the universe vary widely, and not all worldviews attribute creation to divine design. The alternative is to accept the scientific theories that abound, such as the Big Bang theory and evolutionary biology, which seek to explain the origins and development of the universe and life as we know it through natural processes without invoking a supernatural creator.

It is for this reason that John, at the very beginning of his gospel, seeks to eradicate all doubt as to who Jesus is – 'The creator of the universe.'

In the beginning was the Word, and the Word was with God, and the Word was God. He was in the beginning with God. All things were made through Him, and without Him nothing was made that was made. (Jn 1:1-3)

As the creator of all things, He becomes the creator and maker of His Kingdom, His world, the realm of which He has complete rule and authority, a kingdom that literally is without end.

He is the image of the invisible God, the firstborn over all creation. For by Him all things were created that are in heaven and that are on earth, visible and invisible, whether thrones or dominions or principalities or powers. All things were created through Him and for Him. (Col 1:15-16)

The amazing truth is that Jesus has chosen to share the governance of His Kingdom with us. We actually get to reign and rule with Him, here and now. It is why, as 'King of Kings' and our 'High Priest,' He has made us kings and priests and entrusted to us the establishment and expansion of His Kingdom, which one day will cover the earth and stand forever. (Dan 2:44)

But you are a chosen generation, a royal priesthood, a holy nation, His own special people, that you may proclaim the praises of Him who called you out of darkness into His marvellous light; who once were not a people but are now the people of God, who had not obtained mercy but now have obtained mercy. (1 Pet 2:9-10)

Reflection notes by Dele Olowu

The Lord Jesus's main message when He was on earth was essentially the gospel of the kingdom (Mk 1:15; Mt 6:9-10, 33). This gospel, or good news, focused on two main things: the King and His Domain, from which the word 'kingdom' was coined. The Wise Men or astrologers who came from the East (modern-day Iran) to worship this great King while He was still only a baby confirm that He is indeed the Magnificent King of all kings as His influence continues to cause great shakings around the world, two millennia after His departure.

This devotion focuses on who this Magnificent Jesus was and is. Also, on those, He chose to be 'kings and priests' and what this means for all those who called themselves Christians or are called by that name. To illustrate the above points, we highlight how ' kings and priests' have continued to impact the Lord's king-dom agenda in Europe and the rest of the world.

Finally, if space permits, we shall highlight how the enemy who has consistently fought His church since its formation and how to ensure he continues to lose in this battle as the Lord predicted. Mt. 16. 18.

Christ's Identity as King

The prophecy that announced the coming of the Messiah made clear that the government would be on His shoulders and that there shall be no end to His kingdom (Is. 9:6-7). This prophecy about the Lord Jesus Christ has been fulfilled to the letter, even though it was the reason the Romans who ruled Palestine at time, executed Him (Jn. 18:33-37). Considering that the Lord was born into abject poverty, with His earthly parents not having the resources or relations to secure a hotel, motel, or house for the birth of their first child, it is outstanding that He managed to found or establish the largest movement that commands the allegiance of almost 3.4 billion of the world's nearly 8 billion population. One of the clearest explanations for this outcome was/is the kind of people He called and made kings and priests (Rev. 1:6, 5:9-12) and the manner in which they have discharged their portfolios to date.

Maker of Kings and Priests

The Magnificent Jesus chose ordinary people—fishermen, a tax collector, and other peasants—as His followers. He told them to follow Him and trained them to become His apostles (leaders) after his death and resurrection. None of them qualified either by inheritance or conquest to be kings at all, let alone combine the positions of kings and priests, as He Himself and two other famous kings we read about in the Old Testament were described—Melchizedek and David (Gen. 14:18; 2 Sam. 6:14). The ones the Lord Jesus called to be kings and priests, or rulers in the secular and spiritual spheres, were indeed sinners who turned from darkness to light after His blood washed them. They became the propagators of the gospel of His kingdom. Until the proof of the risen Christ was verified, the apostles did not believe He was the promised King and Priest to Israel. Once they were convinced that He indeed still exercised all authority on earth and heaven as He had declared to them after His death and resurrection, they went everywhere to declare His gospel or good news of the kingdom (Mt. 28:18-20; Mk. 16:20). Heb. 2:4 and the Acts of the Apostles and the epistles provide ample proof that He continues to live forever. We are still seeing these in ministries around the world today, led by modern-day leaders of His church. Within only four centuries, the powerful Roman Empire bowed to the gospel of Christ. How was this feat accomplished? By faith in the Risen Christ, prayers, fasting, and a readiness to suffer for the cause if necessary. Missions went out to all corners of the world and are still going out today. Like their King, the kings and priests confirmed the sanctity of their cause by their sacrificial and exemplary lifestyle of simplicity and love for God and man. But the enemy did not give up easily and fought back gallantly.

Satanic Response to the Gospel and where we are today

As the Lord's disciples took hold of all the major pillars of the societies they entered: education, media, entertainment, governance, family, and economy, using the church as her instrumentality, the enemy fought back. The Lord's Kings and Priests used the authority delegated to them by their Master and their diversified gifts to carry out their Lord's command to 'Occupy' till He returned. (see Lk. 19. 11-13). However, as he did in ancient

Israel, Satan made God's people to despise the rock of their salvation (Deut. 32. 15-16) as they grew rich and prosperous. They even embraced strange gods that they had left to turn to Christ initially. Europe provides one of the best illustrations of this today. (read Acts 16 and 17). Thankfully, the wave of revival is being ushered by the fresh thrusts of the Holy Spirit, who is bringing a wind of change as promised.

God's people are being brought from all corners of the world to re-Christianise a people who once led the rest of the world in the gospel. Indeed, exciting days of revival and reformation of the European nations are underway. We must renew our determination to work together, just like the early disciples, to use all of our secular and spiritual gifts across nationalities, tribes, tongues, races, and even denominations. See Acts 13:1-5.

Your Notes

Contemplate Jesus' characteristic highlighted in this chapter. Note down your findings below.

- Agreement: Jesus, You are the maker of kings and priests
- Revelation: Lord, reveal Yourself to me as the maker of kings and priests. Tell me more about this. Unveil more of your plans!
- Keep it: Lord, I commit myself to you as the maker of kings and priests. Help me, Holy Spirit. I dedicate myself and ask for your help. Make me a king and priest. Teach me. I want to work with you.

Glory and power belongs to You forever

"
There are
no large,
complicated
words.
"

...to him be the glory and the power forever and ever. Amen (Revelation 1:6)

Prayer: Lord, today, bring me to the place where I can truly worship You in spirit and in truth.

As Christ is revealed, how can we not do anything else but worship the one who is 'The Magnificent Jesus' with fanatical devotion? This will be a day of worship, Hallelujah!

As we gaze into heaven and observe the throne room, it is obvious who the main character is. Truly to Him belongs all honour and power and glory, forever and forever. He is the famous one, the darling of heaven, our shining star, and everything that Isaiah describes - Wonderful, Counsellor, the Mighty God, and Prince of Peace.

This is why, throughout the Bible, there is a call for the people of God to worship 'The Christ of Heaven.'

> *Then I heard every creature in heaven and on earth and under the earth and on the sea, and all that is in them, saying: 'To him who sits on the throne and to the lamb be praise and honor and glory and power, for ever and ever!' (Rev. 5:13)*

All of creation exists to worship, which is why worship is so important to the emotional nature of the human race. There are many reasons why mankind desires to worship, which may be because of cultural tradition, seeking divine favour, moral guidance, or even as a result of cultural control. All of these the devil will seek to exploit and, as a result is, false and demonic. We, however, as the children of God, are the custodians of true worship to the one and only living God. It is our privilege, honour, passion, and ultimate desire to give Him every ounce of our being in worship.

But the hour is coming, and now is, when the true worshipers will worship the Father in spirit and truth; for the Father is seeking such to worship Him. God is Spirit, and those who worship Him must worship in spirit and truth."
(Jn 4:23-24)

Yes, this will truly be a day of worship! Not the worship of celebrities, sports teams, or mere personalities, but no, it will be a day when my heart joins with the whole of creation to worship Him who is worthy – **The Magnificent Jesus**.

For you shall go out with joy, And be led out with peace; The mountains and the hills shall break forth into singing before you, and all the trees of the field shall clap their hands. (Is 55:12)

In Luke 19:37-40, Jesus says that if people don't worship Him and remain silent, the very stones will immediately cry out.
The act of worshipping Almighty God is deeply ingrained in the human heart and has been present through the corridors of time and throughout the pages of the bible. Maybe today is the day for you to return to the place of worship and repent for what you have made. We simply cannot allow the stones, trees, and fields to take our place.

Reflection notes by Dean Briggs

If you permit me, I want to show you how to make the most of every verse of Scripture as you read this devotional, how to mine it for riches that might otherwise be missed or skimmed over. No doubt you've heard this cluster of words many times — "To Him be the glory and the power forever and ever" — probably having prayed or sung them in some form or another, perhaps as a doxology, or whispered under your breath in worship. The phrasing is so simple and familiar. There are no large, complicated words. The idea is straightforward. And yet, there is a vastness and precision in these twelve words that beg further contemplation. Ponder with me.

Let's begin with the word "be." Consider the simplicity of this imperative. Contrary to our expectations, it is the action verb of the statement. In English, "be" generally indicates the passive form of another verb. Yet here, there is no other verb associated with it. Why? Perhaps this is because all the potential kinetic energy of other verbs is being jealously reserved for what our attention must be directed toward. Furthermore, could it also be that there are no other fitting words with which to narrow down the necessary, all-encompassing broadness of the command? In fact, nearly any other verb placed alongside would likely make the story about what *we* are to do to accomplish the thing that "be" is pointing to. Be loud? Be quiet? Be focused upon? Directing the reader to any action on our part would take away the relentless, all-consuming focus on the only one who can receive the full attention to which these twelve words point. Friends, this journey of discovery you have set upon isn't about you or me at all. Pure and simple, it is about the One who was, is, and is to come. It is about the never-more-to-die, resurrected perpetuity of His stature, His *be*ing.

He. Alone. Full stop.

Thus, all that can be done is to agree with what must be true in relation to Him. And what must be? Glory and power are what must be. *All* glory and all power. This is what *must be* seen as belonging to Him *regardless of anything we do*. And for that very reason — for His preexistent, total worthiness — we can respond to the command in our own small, pitiful, necessary ways. We can worship. We can adore. We can fall down, shout, and be dumbstruck. In some way, these actions on our part can be seen as commensurate or valuable to the degree to which they reflect what is already true. But it is important to acknowledge that this statement removes all doubt: our actions *do not make them true*. We do not add to His worthiness; we merely acknowledge it.

This is why the statement must be broad and, in a sense, passive enough to encompass its desired outcome in such a manner that nothing is spent outside of the centre point of the action: the risen Christ. The command is not passive, but there is nothing we can add to it except our amen. Even our highest praise adds nothing to His worthiness. Every reasonable action we can take — and there are many! — still renders us passive relative to His objective splendour. All of Creation may bear witness and does, but everything in creation is merely window dressing, with every window pointing to the Sonrise. The blinding brilliance of our gaze will finally find its zenith: **in Him!**

Therefore, *to Him* be glory and power! It can be no other way.

If glory and power could be compared to a mighty river crashing and growing through time, then such a river must gather and culminate somewhere. They must have a worthy recipient, a necessary summation. When the most majestic symphony finishes, the rapt crowd of awed attendees has no choice: they stand, roar, and cheer. They have no thought for their place in the story, except to give the beauty of the music the accolade it deserves...

- Christ, the perfect music of heaven.
- Unending song of the Father.
- Logos of God.
- Word made flesh.

- Kinsman Redeemer.
- Lord of Hosts.
- Lamb Who Was Slain.
- Lion of Judah.

The rest of the Revelation of John will unfold, reveal, confirm, and elevate what 65 previous books and thousands of years of documentation in history, prophecy, poetry, and doctrine have already confirmed. But every story has an ending. The summary matters. The last chapter. The final flourish in the great drama of the Eternal Plan.

- The Lamb is on a throne.
- He is seated in perfection. His work is finished.
- He is our eternal High Priest.
- He is the Apostle of our Confession.
- He is the Beloved of the Bride, blazing from head to toe with the fire of His love for us.
- He is Lord Sabaoth, the Champion of Heaven, ready and eager to return and set all things right...

He is the final realisation of every good and perfect thing. If there is any worthy thought, noble value, hope, dream, or goodness, it originates and culminates in Him.

Therefore, it is only fitting for every tributary in the gushing river of history — all the majesties of redemption, every virtue of praise, every witness embedded in the created order, including the endless fascination of angels and wonder-struck awe of humanity — *to Him and none other do these things flow.* Therefore, to HIM, glory and honour must be given.

Lastly, notice that even though the imperative of these twelve words is present tense — hear the **nowness**; not yesterday, not tomorrow — yet in the paradox and mystery of God's infinitide, the present glory of Christ must be recognised as *eternally* relevant. His stature and status as the Worthy One will never change, diminish, subside, or be comparable to another. John declares: now to Him…be glory and honour…**forever and ever**.

No, this is not a doxology you peg onto the end of a prayer. This is a manifesto that will never end. And for this reason, even after declaring it, John can only add the necessary, emphatic echo: Amen! This is so true, and John restates his and our corporate agreement. Let it be! *(This is what the Greek word Amen means.)*

Yes, we agree. Let His glory *be!*

Your Notes

Contemplate Jesus' characteristic highlighted in this chapter.
Note down your findings below.

- Agreement: Jesus, all glory and power belongs to you forever and ever
- Revelation: Lord, reveal Yourself to me as the most glorious and powerful. Tell me more about this. Tell me, what is it like to have all the power in heaven and on earth?
- Keep it: Lord, I commit myself to you. Help me, Holy Spirit. I want to worship Jesus. I dedicate myself as a worshipper and ask for your help. Overwhelm me with your glory and power.

CHAPTER 10

Every eye will see You

> You will draw
all men
to Yourself.

Prayer Lord, I pray that you will make us ready for your return and keep us watchful, for we know neither the day nor the hour in which you, the Son of Man, is coming.

> *Behold, He is coming with clouds, and every eye will see Him, even they who pierced Him. And all the tribes of the earth will mourn because of Him. Even so, Amen. (Rev 1:7)*

What an amazing statement this is - that every eye will see Him!! Jesus, the 'Christ,' will be seen by all when He returns, and it will be the biggest event to ever take place since the creation of the world.

> *Then the sign of the Son of Man will appear in heaven, and then all the tribes of the earth will mourn, and they will see the Son of Man coming on the clouds of heaven with power and great glory. (Matt 24:30)*

Jesus is coming again, there is no doubt, but what if we knew for certain that he would be coming tonight? Would we live any differently? I suspect that the answer to that question would be "Absolutely Yes." Someone once said that we should plan our lives as if we were to live for a thousand years and live our lives as if Jesus were to come again at any moment.

It is not easy to imagine what the coming of the Lord will look like. Quite simply, it will be beyond our wildest imaginations. All we know is that which Paul talked about when he wrote to the Corinthians, explaining to them that presently, we only see reflections in a dull mirror. However, there is coming a time when we will see everything clearly, just as God sees us, and I personally believe it will be when Jesus returns, and every single person will have a vantage point as 'The Christ of Heaven' – 'The Magnificent Jesus' is revealed in all of His glory.

> *We don't yet see things clearly. We're squinting in a fog, peering through a mist. But it won't be long before the weather clears and the sun shines bright! We'll see it all then, see it all as clearly as God sees us, knowing him directly just as he knows us! (1 Cor 13:12 MSG)*

In the meantime, we continue to glean from Scripture what we think this earth-shattering event might be like. We get some help from Daniel's book, as he describes his night vision and the profound effect it had on him.

> *"In my night visions, I saw that with the clouds of heaven came someone who looked like a man. He approached the old sage and was led before him. Power, honour, and kingdom were bestowed upon him, and all peoples and nations, whatever language they spoke, served him. His reign was an eternal reign that would never end. His kingdom would never be destroyed.*
> *(Dan 7:13-15)*

This is going to be the most seismic moment in world history, incomparable and unparalleled to anything else. Daniel caught a glimpse of that which the whole of mankind will experience in its fullness.

Soon, the world will see **The Magnificent Jesus** shrouded in glory and shining like the sun. We will see Him, the one who has loved us before time itself.

In that moment, we will love Him and yet fear Him, which will cause us to bend the knee and bow before Him as He is acknowledged by everyone as Lord of Lord and King of Kings.

Reflection notes by Carolyn Jones

Jesus, You said of Yourself and Your mission to the world: " And I, if I be lifted up from the earth, will draw all men unto Myself" (John 12:32). This was not an easy thing for You to say. You admitted publicly, "Now my soul has become troubled." At that moment, it looks like You had to walk Yourself through Your mission and where You stood in relation to the Father's existence and glory. Did You experience that intrinsic human struggle with self-preservation? An existential crisis? As You saw events coming to a climax, the hard choice became real, and it took nothing less than the audible voice of God to comfort and encourage You. The stakes, apparently, could not have been higher. What was at stake? The plan of salvation itself: the glory of the Father in drawing all men to You on the cross.

Draw.

The pull of the cross's spectacle of horror and love combined is powerful and relentless, but one we can resist. Ultimately, we also have a choice to make. The pull is always there – yet other things pull on us as well – our own sense of self and the immediacy of life filling our senses. You know this as no one else in heaven does because You stood in our shoes; You know how that feels. We know that You know. You identified with us, and we identify with You and are drawn to You, but You do not force us to come. You prophesied that when You would be lifted up, You would 'draw all men' to Yourself.

This is the mystery of prophecy: it is truth, Your word creates the possibility, and it is something to lay hold of by faith when the opposite seems to be happening. It is a promise made by a trustworthy, credible person who has all the ability to fulfil it – it is not just a simple prediction. You are actively involved in fulfilling Your word, not simply stating a future fact. So, the very people who rejected and betrayed You – Your own Jewish people – who *had to* reject You to bring about Your crucifixion, were yet included in Your word of prophecy: they, as all men, will ultimately be drawn to You.

Today, we still wait for that prophecy to come to completion – and never in the intervening 1900 years has it been easier to see that it could happen, is happening, and is so tantalisingly close. The day when all eyes will see You, even those who pierced You, and they will mourn for You as for an only Son. All Israel will be saved. And Your word will become reality, that when You are lifted high, You will draw all men to Yourself.

Your Notes

Contemplate Jesus' characteristic highlighted in this chapter.
Note down your findings below.

- Agreement: Jesus, Every eye will see You.
- Revelation: Holy Spirit, Tell me more about this. Unveil more of this moment, that every eye will see You. Do you look forward to this moment?
- Keep it: Lord, I commit myself to this day. I expected you on the clouds. I look forward to your arrival. Help me, Holy Spirit. I dedicate myself and ask for your help. Overwhelm me by the impact of this special day!

Conclusion

As we draw this first volume of The Magnificent Jesus to a close, it is essential to reflect on the profound insights we have uncovered about the nature of Jesus Christ and the transformative power of intimacy with Him. Throughout this book, we have delved into the richness of His character, exploring His many attributes as revealed in the book of Revelation. Each chapter has opened a window into a different aspect of who Jesus is—His love, His faithfulness, His authority, and His eternal presence.

The journey to know Christ is a pilgrimage that transcends mere knowledge or understanding. It is a call to deeper intimacy, where our relationship with Him becomes the foundation of our lives. Jesus invites us into a relationship that is not just based on religious practice but on a genuine, personal connection with the living God. This is a relationship marked by trust, devotion, and the daily experience of His presence.

The revelation of Jesus as the Christ of Heaven is not just a theological concept but a living reality that transforms our lives. As we gaze upon Him, we are changed; as we walk with Him, we are empowered. The intimacy we cultivate with Jesus is not an end in itself but the means by which His glory is revealed in us and through us to the world.

While this book marks the completion of Volume 1, our journey is far from over. This is only the beginning of a deeper exploration into the magnificent character of Jesus Christ. In the upcoming Volumes 2 and 3, we will continue to unveil more of the treasures hidden in Him, delving further into the mysteries of His person and the power of His presence.

Each volume will build upon the foundation laid here, guiding us into even greater depths of understanding and intimacy with our Saviour. As you look forward to these future volumes, let the insights you have gained from this first volume lead you to a deeper, more intimate relationship with the Magnificent Jesus, and may His glory be reflected in every area of your life.

Closing Prayer

Lord Jesus, we thank You for revealing Yourself to us through Your Word and through the insights shared in this book. My heart is overflowing with gratitude, awe, and reverence for You. Thank You for Your incredible qualities that never cease to astonish us. Jesus, You are the one who is, who was, and who is to come. With an all-encompassing view, You see everything, and before Your throne stand seven spirits, the complete and powerful presence of the Holy Spirit. You are the faithful witness, the solid rock of stability and assurance. You are the firstborn from the dead, supreme in all things, and how wonderful it is that You hold that position. You are the ruler over the kings of the earth, and one day, every knee will bow before You. Jesus, You love us deeply, and we want to fully embrace that love once more today. You have freed us from our sins through Your blood, making us truly free. You have established a kingdom of priests, thank You for this beautiful plan. One day, everyone will see You, and what a profound and unique moment that will be. All glory and power are Yours, forever and ever. We worship You. As we conclude this first volume, we ask that You continue to draw us closer to You. Help us to live in the fullness of Your love and to walk in the power of Your Spirit. May our lives be a testimony to Your greatness, and may we always seek to know You more deeply. Prepare our hearts for the revelations yet to come, and let our journey with You grow ever richer in the days ahead.
Amen.

Biography

Johan den Hartogh (The Netherlands)

Johan den Hartogh is married to Hannah, and they have four children together. They reside in The Hague, The Netherlands. Johan is the founder of the foundation 24-7Prayer in the Netherlands and the foundation Justice House of Prayer in The Hague, both of which are dedicated to fostering continuous prayer and justice through faith-based initiatives. Johan's primary calling is to bring people closer to God, helping them deepen their spiritual lives. That is the reason he wrote this book.

In addition to his work in ministry, he is actively engaged in the business world, where he strives to exemplify and promote the values of God's Kingdom in the workplace. His dual focus on faith and enterprise underscores his commitment to integrating spirituality with everyday life, encouraging others to live out their beliefs in all areas of their lives.

Ken Gott (England)

Ken has been married to Lois for 48 years, and they have three married daughters and nine grandchildren. Ken Gott lives in the *'City of Sunderland'* in Northeast England, where he gives apostolic oversight to the region and beyond. Ken is also the founder of the 'House of Prayer Europe' and 'This is the Kingdom,' which promotes, trains, and equips the 'Body of Christ' for

Kingdom expansion as cities are transformed and nations discipled. Having been in full-time ministry for over 39 years, which saw him actively participating in many major spiritual renewal movements, he now passionately desires to see the church awakened by the 'Fire of God' and fulfil its ultimate purpose.

About the Contributors

Lou Engle (United States)

Lou Engle is an intercessor for revival, and the visionary co-founder of TheCall, a prayer and fasting movement responsible for gathering hundreds of thousands around the globe.

He has been involved in church planting, establishing prayer movements and strategic houses of prayer. He is the founder of the pro-life ministry Bound4Life. Now residing in Colorado Springs, he is married to his beautiful wife Therese and blessed with 7 wonderful children. He is the president of Lou Engle Ministries, recently launched to mobilise fasting and contending prayer, and to envision and empower stadium christianity, and to ignite reformation prayer into the nations of the earth.

Luke Finch (Scotland)

A worship pastor for over 20 years both in England and the United States and leading worship internationally at conferences and large festivals. Luke is a gifted songwriter who has released four albums and has been featured on almost twenty worship albums. The Revelation Room's album was released last year in collaboration with GPA Worship. That's the professional stuff, but Luke is a family man all day, every day. He and his wife, Deborah live in Ayrshire, Scotland.

Sarah-Jane Biggart (Scotland)

Sarah-Jane, quite simply, is one who loves the Lord, yields to Him daily, and aims to follow the Holy Spirit's leading in all she does. Her heart is to 'do the work of the one who sends her' and 'only do what she sees the Father doing. Sarah-Jane, with a background in corporate business, has spent 15 years in full-time ministry. She is a seasoned prophet with a passion for the 'Word,' worship, and prayer. Her focus in seeking the Lord is to understand, learn, and follow His ways. Working with Him in authentic, relational collaboration with others to see the Kingdom come and the Body of Christ flourish through oneness in Him. She has written 'Seeing Beyond,' a practical book to help equip the church to be victorious, activating us to see and sense the spirit realm daily.

SJ is married with two adult children. She lives with her husband in beautiful Perthshire, Scotland.

Wes Hall (United States)

A former corporate lawyer from the UK, Wes Hall has been teaching the Bible for almost thirty years. Currently based in Florida, He has served a number of ministries and churches in the UK, Germany, and the USA over the last twenty-five years, pioneering several ministry schools. He is passionate about men and women discovering their identity in Christ and being equipped in the Word of God and by the power of the Spirit to impact the nations with the Gospel. He is married to Carol, and they have four children together. More information at awakeinternational.org.

Duncan Smith (United States)

Duncan and his wife Kate, carry the fire of God, His love, power, and revival all over the world. Together, they serve as the Presidents of 'Catch The Fire World', a global network of revival churches, missions, and ministries birthed out of the Toronto Revival.

Based in Raleigh, North Carolina, USA, they apostolically oversee the leadership team of Catch The Fire, Raleigh, a vibrant, growing church full of the love and presence of God. Their passion is to extend the 'Kingdom of God' by planting and cultivating supernatural churches, ministries, and missions in multiple expressions and multiple generations. Wherever they go, the Holy Spirit does extraordinary miracles, as the love of the Father and the grace of Jesus is poured out to the world.

Franklyn Spence (Switzerland)

Franklyn is the founder of Forerunner Ministries and God's Masterclass in Basle, Switzerland. He is the author of" Point of the Spear, The Essential Guide to Prophetic Intercession and Spiritual Warfare" and also "Breakthrough to a Supernatural Life, Keys to Hearing God's Voice."

Franklyn is the European Ambassador for the International Coalition of Prophetic Leaders. He also runs courses and speaks at conferences worldwide, sharing his journey of loving the Lord and experiencing the power of the Holy Spirit.

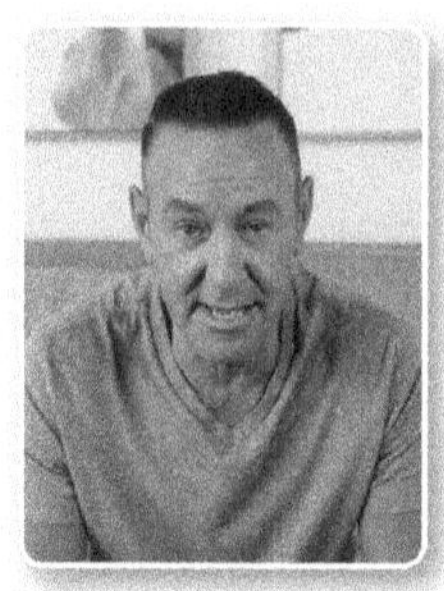

Murray Hiebert (United States)

Murray Hiebert is married to Deborah, and they are the founders of OneEleven. It's a global mission movement that equips nations for night and day worship, prayer, and missions. We believe gospel proclamation with worship and prayer will revive the church and usher in a great harvest of souls in every place. Today, the Lord is unfolding great work to make us a house of prayer for all nations. OneEleven joins the epic unfolding of God's redemptive plan by making disciples, training leaders, and sending missionaries. Murray and Deborah give themselves tirelessly to see the global church strengthened in her identity as a House of Prayer for all nations. Their home base is in Kansas City, but you can often find them overseas with their family training and equipping leaders for night & day worship & prayer.

Steve Uppal (England)

Alongside his wife, Esther, Steve has been the senior leader of All Nations Church since 2001. Steve is also recognised as the Apostolic leader of the growing All Nations Movement, which gathers churches and leaders with the vision of turning nations back to God through prayer, disciple-making, and church planting. Steve's passion is for the church to fulfil her glorious destiny and for every believer to become strong in their inner being, engage with God's purpose and find their place in His plans. He is also an author; among his books are Revival Ready, Rousing the Warriors, and Highly Flammable. Steve and Esther have four grown children, three of whom are now married. They are enjoying grandparenting!

John Arnott (Canada)

John Arnott and his wife Carol have spent over thirty-five years ministering in the anointing and shepherding revival and are also the founders of the 'Catch The Fire Network of Churches.'

As international speakers, John and Carol, in the context of the Father's saving and restoring Love, have carried Revival to the five continents of the world. As the Holy Spirit moves with signs and wonders, they have seen millions of lives touched and changed through God's power and Christ's love.

Dele Olowu (The Netherlands)

Pastor Dele Olowu is presently the Special Assistant to the General Overseer (SATGO), Europe Mainland Affairs. He has taught and researched public policy issues (the areas in which he has a doctorate) in several African countries, Canada, America, and Europe. He advises several governments and international organisations on development and policy improvement matters. He has pastored churches in Nigeria, Ethiopia, Tunisia, and the Netherlands. He lives in Dordrecht (NL) with his wife. They together have three children and two grandchildren. As part of his portfolio, he directly oversees the countries in Europe of RCCG.

Dean Briggs (United States)

Dean Briggs is married to Jeanie, the father of eight grown children and presently grandfather to six. A former pastor and church planter, Dean is now a sought-after Bible teacher who serves the Body of Christ as an apostolic teacher and strategist, consulting movements, ministries, and coaching leaders and executives across five continents with a powerful message concerning sonship, righteousness, Ekklesia reformation, and revival. He is the author of numerous fiction and non-fiction books, whose titles include Ekklesia Rising and The Great Communion Revival. He and his wife, Jeanie, reside in Kansas City, MO.

Carolyn Jones (The Netherlands)

Carolyn Jones is married to Mark and lives in Zoetermeer, The Netherlands. Carolyn is originally from New Zealand. She is the former director of the European English Aglow. She is passionate about strengthening others in their faith.

Overview of Citations

p. 14   But you, when you pray, go into your (inner) room, and when you have shut your door, ***pray to your Father who is in the secret place***; (Matthew 6:6)

p. 16   When Jesus came into the region of Caesarea Philippi, He asked His disciples, saying, "Who do men say that I, the Son of Man, am?" So they said, "Some say John the Baptist, some Elijah, and others Jeremiah or one of the prophets." He said to them, "But who do you say that I am?" Simon Peter answered and said, "You are the Christ, the Son of the living God." Jesus answered and said to him, "Blessed are you, Simon Bar-Jonah, for flesh and blood has not revealed this to you, but My Father who is in heaven. And I also say to you that you are Peter, and on this rock I will build My church, and the gates of Hades shall not prevail against it. And I will give you the keys of the kingdom of heaven, and whatever you bind on earth will be bound in heaven, and whatever you loose on earth will be loosed in heaven." Then He commanded His disciples that they should tell no one that He was Jesus the Christ. (Matt 16:13-20)

p. 19   "And I will give you the keys of the kingdom of heaven, and whatever you bind on earth will be bound in heaven, and whatever you loose on earth will be loosed in heaven." (Matthew 16:19)

p. 20   "For now we see in a mirror, dimly, but then face to face. Now I know in part, but then I shall know just as I also am known". (1 Corinthians 13:12)

p. 20   "Eye has not seen, nor ear heard, nor have entered into the heart of man, the things which God has prepared for those who love Him." (1 Corinthians 2:9)

p. 20   "Beloved, now we are children of God; and it has not yet been revealed what we shall be, but we know that when He is revealed, we shall be like Him, for we shall see Him as He is." (1 John 3:2)

p. 29   The Revelation of Jesus Christ, which God gave Him to show His servants—things which must shortly take place. And He sent and signified it by His angel to His servant John, who bore witness to the word of God, and to the testimony of Jesus Christ, to all things that he saw. Blessed is he who reads and those who hear the words of this prophecy, and keep those things which are written in it; for the time is near. (Rev 1:1-3)

p. 30   Blessed is the man who reads aloud the word of this prophecy; and blessed are those who hear [it read] and who keep themselves true to the things which are written in it [heeding them and laying them to heart], for the time [for them to be fulfilled] is near. (Revelation 1:3 Amp)

p. 30   Blessed is the man Who walks not in the counsel of the ungodly, Nor stands in the path of sinners, Nor sits in the seat of the scornful; But his delight is in the law of the LORD, And in His law he meditates day and night. (Ps 1:1-2)

p. 31   He who testifies to these things says, "Surely I am coming quickly." Amen. Even so, come, Lord Jesus! (Revelation 22:20)

p. 31   ....that the God of our Lord Jesus Christ, the Father of glory, may give to you the spirit of wisdom and revelation in the knowledge of Him, the eyes of your understanding being enlightened; that you may know what is the hope of His calling, what are the riches of the glory of His inheritance in the saints, and what is the exceeding greatness of His power toward us who believe, according to the working of His mighty power. (Ephesians 1:17-19)

p. 31   The king answered Daniel, and said, "Truly your God is the God of gods, the Lord of kings, and a revealer of secrets, since you could reveal this secret." (Daniel 2:47)

p. 33   He is the image of the invisible God, the firstborn over all creation. For by Him all things were created that are in heaven and that are on earth, visible and invisible, whether thrones or dominions or principalities or powers. All things were created through Him and for Him. And He is before all things, and in Him all things consist (Colossians 1:15-17)

p. 33   I will tell you of new things of hidden things unknown to you. They are created now and not long ago; you have not heard of them before today. (Isaiah 48:6)

p. 34   "Very truly I tell you," Jesus answered, "before Abraham was born, I am!" (John 8:58)

p. 34   **Word in the beginning** In the beginning was the Word, and the Word was with God, and the Word was God. He was in the beginning with God. All things were made through Him, and without Him nothing was made that was made. In Him was life, and the life was the light of men. And the light shines in the darkness, and the darkness did not comprehend it. (John 1:1-5)

p. 39   These are the words of him who holds the seven spirits of God. (Rev:3:1)

p. 39   From the throne came flashes of lightning, rumblings and peals of thunder. In front of the throne, seven lamps were blazing. These are the seven spirits of God. (Rev:4-5)

p. 39   Then I saw a Lamb, looking as if it had been slain, standing at the centre of the throne, encircled by the four living creatures and the elders. The Lamb had seven horns and seven eyes, which are the seven spirits of God sent out into all the earth. (Rev 5:6)

p. 41   "Nevertheless, I have this against you, that you have left your first love. Remember therefore from where you have fallen; repent and do the first works, or else I will come to you quickly and remove your lampstand from its place—unless you repent". (Rev 2:4)

p. 43   For the eyes of the LORD run to and fro throughout the whole earth, to show Himself strong on behalf of those whose heart is loyal to Him. In this you have done foolishly; therefore from now on you shall have wars." (2 Chronicles 16:9)

p. 50   Again, a new commandment I write to you, which thing is true in Him and in you, because the darkness is passing away, and the true light is already shining. (1 Jn 2:8)

p. 51   Greater love has no one than this, than to lay down one's life for his friends. (John 15:13)

p. 51   But God demonstrates His own love toward us, in that while we were still sinners, Christ died for us. (Romans 5:8)

p. 52   'They triumphed over him by the blood of the Lamb and by the word of their testimony; they did not love their lives so much as to shrink from death.' (Revelation 12:11)

p. 52   But he, full of the Holy Spirit, gazed into Heaven and saw the glory of God and Jesus (as the 'Faithful Witness') standing at the right hand of God. And he said, "Behold I see the Heavens opened and the Son of Man standing at the right hand of God." (Acts 7:55-56)

p. 52   "Lord Jesus, receive my spirit" and falling to his knees he cried out with a loud voice, "Lord do not hold this sin against them." (Acts 7:59-60)

p. 62   He is the image of the invisible God, the firstborn over all creation. For by Him all things were created that are in heaven and that are on earth, visible and invisible, whether thrones or dominions or principalities or powers. All things were created through Him and for Him. And He is before all things, and in Him all things consist. And He is the head of the body, the church, who is the beginning, the firstborn from the dead, that in all things He may have the pre-eminence. (Col 1:15-18)

p. 62   And we know that all things work together for good to those who love God, to those who are the called according to His purpose. For whom He foreknew, He also predestined to be conformed to the image of His Son, that He might be the firstborn among many brethren. (Rom 8:28-29)

p. 63   "I refuse to live an ordinary Christian life when I serve and am filled with an extraordinary God."

p. 63   And He is the head of the body, the church, who is the beginning, the firstborn from the dead, that in all things He may have the pre-eminence. (Colossians 1:18)

p. 64   Most assuredly, I say to you, unless a grain of wheat falls into the ground and dies, it remains alone; but if it dies, it produces much grain. (John 12:24)

p. 64   Then He spoke many things to them in parables, saying: "Behold, a Sower went out to sow. And as he sowed, some seed fell by the wayside ...... Some fell on stony places..... And some fell among thorns.... But others fell on good ground and yielded a crop: some a hundredfold, some sixty, some thirty. (Matthew 13:1-9)

p. 65 But if the Spirit of Him who raised Jesus from the dead dwells in you, He who raised Christ from the dead will also give life to your mortal bodies through His Spirit who dwells in you. (Romans 8:11)

p. 65 This charge I commit to you, son Timothy, according to the prophecies previously made concerning you, that by them you may wage the good warfare,.... (1 Tim 1:18)

p. 71 ...... The king answered Daniel, and said, "Truly your **God is the God** of gods, the Lord of kings, and a revealer of secrets"..... (Dan 2:47)

p. 72 The seventh angel sounded his trumpet, and there were loud voices in heaven, which said: "The kingdom of the world has become the kingdom of our Lord and of his Messiah, and he will reign for ever and ever." (Revelation 11:15)

p. 72 For it is written: "As I live, says the LORD, Every knee shall bow to Me, And every tongue shall confess to God." (Rom 14:11)

p. 72 ...He raised Him from the dead and seated Him at His right hand in the heavenly places, far above all principality and power and might and dominion, and every name that is named, not only in this age but also in that which is to come. And He put all things under His feet, and gave Him to be head over all things to the church, which is His body, the fullness of Him who fills all in all.(Eph. 1:20-23)

p. 72 Finally, there is laid up for me the crown of righteousness, which the Lord, the righteous Judge, will give to me on that Day, and not to me only but also to all who have loved His appearing. (2 Tim 4:8)

p. 79   But God demonstrates His own love toward us, in that while we
were still sinners, Christ died for us. (Rom 5:8)

p. 79   For I am persuaded that neither death nor life, nor angels nor principalities nor powers, nor things present nor things to come, nor height
nor depth, nor any other created thing, shall be able to separate us from
the love of God which is in Christ Jesus our Lord. (Rom 8:38-39)

p. 80   You have ravished my heart, my sister, my spouse; you have ravished my heart with one look of your eyes, with one link of your
necklace.(Songs 4:9)

p. 80   And we are His portion, and He is our prize Drawn to redemption
by the grace in His eyes If grace is an ocean, we're all sinking So
Heaven meets Earth like an unforeseen kiss And my heart turns
violently inside of my chest I don't have time to maintain these
regrets When I think about the way He loves us

p. 89   Likewise, He also took the cup after supper, saying, "This cup is the
new covenant in My blood, which is shed for you. (Luke 22:20)

p. 89   He went a little farther and fell on His face, and prayed, saying, "O
My Father, if it is possible, let this cup pass from Me; nevertheless,
not as I will, but as You will." (Mat 26:39)

p. 90   In Him, we have redemption through his blood, the forgiveness of
sins, in accordance with the riches of God's grace. (Eph. 1:7)

p. 90   "Come now, and let us reason together, Says the LORD, Though
your sins are like scarlet, They shall be as white as snow; Though
they are red like crimson, They shall be as wool." (Is 1:18)

p. 100   In the beginning was the Word, and the Word was with God, and the Word was God. He was in the beginning with God. All things were made through Him, and without Him nothing was made that was made. (Jn 1:1-3)

p. 100   He is the image of the invisible God, the firstborn over all creation. For by Him all things were created that are in heaven and that are on earth, visible and invisible, whether thrones or dominions or principalities or powers. All things were created through Him and for Him. (Col 1:15-16)

p. 100   But you are a chosen generation, a royal priesthood, a holy nation, His own special people, that you may proclaim the praises of Him who called you out of darkness into His marvellous light; who once were not a people but are now the people of God, who had not obtained mercy but now have obtained mercy. (1 Pet 2:9-10)

p. 109   Then I heard every creature in heaven and on earth and under the earth and on the sea, and all that is in them, saying: 'To him who sits on the throne and to the lamb be praise and honor and glory and power, for ever and ever!' (Rev. 5:13)

p. 110   But the hour is coming, and now is, when the true worshipers will worship the Father in spirit and truth; for the Father is seeking such to worship Him. God is Spirit, and those who worship Him must worship in spirit and truth." (Jn 4:23-24)

p. 110   For you shall go out with joy, And be led out with peace; The mountains and the hills shall break forth into singing before you, and all the trees of the field shall clap their hands. (Is 55:12)

p. 119   Behold, He is coming with clouds, and every eye will see Him, even they who pierced Him. And all the tribes of the earth will mourn because of Him. Even so, Amen. (Rev 1:7)

p. 119   Then the sign of the Son of Man will appear in heaven, and then all the tribes of the earth will mourn, and they will see the Son of Man coming on the clouds of heaven with power and great glory. (Matt 24:30)

p. 120   We don't yet see things clearly. We're squinting in a fog, peering through a mist. But it won't be long before the weather clears and the sun shines bright! We'll see it all then, see it all as clearly as God sees us, knowing him directly just as he knows us! (1 Cor 13:12 MSG)

p. 120   "In my night visions, I saw that with the clouds of heaven came someone who looked like a man. He approached the old sage and was led before him. Power, honour, and kingdom were bestowed upon him, and all peoples and nations, whatever language they spoke, served him. His reign was an eternal reign that would never end. His kingdom would never be destroyed. (Dan 7:13-15)

p. 126   **_Closing Prayer_** Lord Jesus, we thank You for revealing Yourself to us through Your Word and through the insights shared in this book. My heart is overflowing with gratitude, awe, and reverence for You. Thank You for Your incredible qualities that never cease to astonish us. Jesus, You are the one who is, who was, and who is to come. With an all-encompassing view, You see everything, and before Your throne stand seven spirits, the complete and powerful presence of the Holy Spirit. You are the faithful witness, the solid rock of stability and assurance. You are the firstborn from the dead, supreme in all things, and how wonderful it is that You hold that position. You are the ruler over the kings of the earth, and one day, every knee will bow before You. Jesus, You love us deeply, and we want to fully embrace that love once more today. You have freed us from our sins through Your blood, making us truly free. You have established a kingdom of priests, thank You for this beautiful plan. One day, everyone will see You, and what a profound and unique moment that will be. All glory and power are Yours, forever and ever. We worship You. As we conclude this first volume, we ask that You continue to draw us closer to You. Help us to live in the fullness of Your love and to walk in the power of Your Spirit. May our lives be a testimony to Your greatness, and may we always seek to know You more deeply. Prepare our hearts for the revelations yet to come, and let our journey with You grow ever richer in the days ahead.Amen.